The Racing Fords

Also by Hans Tanner

Ferrari

Corvair Guide

Great Racing Drivers of the World

The Racing Fords

by Hans Tanner

MEREDITH PRESS/New York

CONTENTS

INTRODUCTION

The American Challenge

At 4 P.M. on Sunday, June 19, 1966, a trio of Ford racing cars crossed the finish line for the 24 Hours of Le Mans road race, bringing the United States its first victory in the international classic.

Why and how Ford automobiles came to be the American challenge in international competition is a story that began long ago. Ford Motor Company was a power in automobile racing even before racing grew to become America's second biggest spectator sport. The heritage dates back to the company founder, Henry Ford, who early in the century piloted the famed Ford 999 racer to set a world land speed record and capture the imagination of the American public.

The stage was set for the Ford Le Mans program in June, 1962, when Henry Ford II announced Ford Motor Company's withdrawal from the five-year-old Automobile Manufacturers Association agreement to ban racing activities. Three years later Charles H. Patterson was describing the racing policy as "a prudent business investment, being a factor in product improvement and sales record."

Ford had to have a reason for entering automobile racing. These reasons were basically fourfold. A manufacturer's product benefits from the development and usage of new ideas and materials. The exacting requirements of special performance vehicles make them a rich field for innovation, a thorough school for engineering excellence, and an ultimate challenge in quality control. The net result is safer, more reliable, more efficient automotive transportation.

Engineers are afforded a wide range of experience in a concentrated time period. Often it has been said that "racing improves the breed," but this does not apply only to the mechanical aspects of motor vehicles; it also means improving the breed of the engineers, designers, and manufacturing people who adapt the improvements for highway use. From their work on racing cars, these specialists learn more about automobiles—faster and perhaps more painfully— than they could ever have learned otherwise. Open competition is a valuable adjunct to engineering and research facilities and to normal testing operations on proving grounds and public highways. It enables and forces the manufacturer to compress time, mechanical wear, and human experience. It adds to the imponderables of human action and reaction under the stress of competition that no computer can simulate.

An excellent promotional medium is provided by demonstrating products in open competition. Nothing does more to sell a product than respect and enthusiasm for it, nothing generates enthusiasm at a greater rate for a car than winning in flat-out competition. The reverse side of the coin is that losing can hurt a product's reputation, but that is a gamble that the manufacturer must take when he becomes involved in automobile racing.

After reviewing the initial reasons for taking to the racetrack, company officials found that involvement in a racing program has had a marked effect on company morale. After two years of such involvement, Ford officials felt that although they were in business to sell automobiles, not win races, the company morale had been considerably uplifted, that the checkered flag was more dramatic and more stimulating than a 10-day sales report. Some officials feel that this runoff has been the biggest return of all from the racing investment—an obvious increase of "enthusiasm for work" from the assembly lines to the executive suites.

The Racing Fords

CHAPTER 1

The Early Days

Detroit, at the turn of the century, was a city of broad avenues and shaded streets. Along Woodward Avenue merchants lingered on the sidewalks while in rebuilt stables, carpenters' shops, and former carriage works groups of men turned out strange collections of nuts and bolts called automobiles.

The trend of the infant automobile industry was toward speed. Racing was on everyone's mind, and cross-country endurance tests, hill climbs, and track races began to hold the interest of the public.

Everywhere promoters and men with money were looking to enter the new field, either with their money or in person. In many ways it was almost like a gold rush with the bonanza going to those who got in first and were able to stake out the best claims. Sensational stunts were needed to attract the public's eye and nothing lent itself better to this than the big awkward monsters that thundered around the dirt tracks at seemingly breakneck speeds.

That was the situation Henry Ford faced when he rented space in the loft of a shop near the C. R. Wilson Body Company, on Cass Avenue beside the railroad tracks.

Ford's assistant in his experimental work on automobiles was C. Harold Wills, who worked during the day at the Boyer Machine Company and moonlighted with Henry Ford at night. Ford had made up his mind to establish himself so thoroughly with the public that the finding of financial support would be certain and a company could be formed that closely followed his own particular ideas. To achieve this he realized he would have to compete in the racing field, a somewhat hazardous occupation in his opinion, and would have to build a car that was faster than any other one competing. Other men had similar thoughts; Alexander Winton had completed his Bullet and a young Harvard student named Cannon was building a streamlined steamer.

Winton was the best known of America's racing drivers. He had set the first American track record on Decoration Day, 1897, and had achieved additional fame by taking his car to Europe and entering it in a foreign race for the first time. In America he had won almost every race in which he had entered. Clearly, if Henry Ford wanted publicity, he would have to take on Winton. His decision made to tackle the national hero, Ford began drawing up plans, and with the assistance of his mechanic Ed "Spider" Huff, the car was built.

The match race was scheduled for October at the Grosse Point track. The promoters were Daniel Campau, owner of the track, William Metzger, a Detroit bicycle dealer, and Charles B. Shanks, the Winton sales manager. Shanks picked out a beautiful punch bowl set as the sweepstake prize, as he figured it would look well in the bay window of the Winton dining room.

On the night before the race, Henry Ford walked into Metzger's bicycle shop on Woodward Avenue and posted his cash entry fee for the sweepstakes event, and the punch bowl set was destined for a different home than that envisioned by Shanks.

The day of the race dawned dark and gloomy with storm clouds rolling in from the northwest. Despite the threatening weather, a large parade formed in downtown Detroit at 10:30 A.M. and made its way out to the old Grosse Point Blue Ribbon Track.

The parade was headed by mounted police, followed by two steam vehicles pulling a tallyho coach in which a band was blasting away noisily. Court in Detroit was officially adjourned for the afternoon to give the attorneys and others an opportunity to see the racers, and by race time in midafternoon eight thousand spectators were crammed in and the line for tickets was more than a hundred yards long. The local newspapers called it "The World's Championship and the first big race in the West."

Before the main event several preliminary races were run off. A five-mile race for steam cars opened the program and finally the track was cleared for the big event. It was a championship race over a ten-mile course for cars of unrestricted weight.

As the cars were called to the line, three drivers reported—Henry Ford, Winton, and a Pittsburgh millionaire, William N. Murray. As they waited for the start, Murray's mechanic discovered a cylinder leak in the engine and Murray's car had to be withdrawn.

Ford's car was totally unlike Winton's fully developed racer. Winton claimed 40 horsepower while Henry's car was rated at 26. At the starting gun Winton took the lead and was clearly faster than Ford. By the time seven laps had been completed the Winton was almost half a mile ahead. One newspaper reported: "Ford's mechanic hung far out in his effort to ballast the car, but she swung wide at every turn. That Mr. Ford was an amateur was plainly shown by the way he took the curves. At the turns he was compelled to shut off the power entirely and two fifths of the time his machine was simply coasting."

Suddenly and without warning a plume of blue smoke appeared at the tail of the Winton and quickly a big cloud developed. Winton's mechanic was frantically pouring oil on the red-hot bearings of the car's engine. The same scribe reported: "Mr. Ford swept by them as though they were standing still. Down the stretch he came like a demon, and the crowd yelled itself hoarse. In the next three miles Ford increased his lead to fully three-quarters of a mile and won amid great cheering."

Henry Ford covered the 10 miles in 13 minutes and 23 2/5 seconds to take the punch bowl set.

The next day a Detroit newspaper announced Ford's sentiments under the headline "Once Is Enough." The paper continued: "Henry Ford broke into the front ranks of American chauffeurs yesterday, but it is likely that he will never again be seen in a race. This determination to remain out of the races does not mean that Mr. Ford will not go on the track again. On the contrary, he is convinced that his mechanic is capable of making a mile a minute, and he will go after the record." Ford was quoted as saying that Winton in Ford's car could beat anything in the country.

The day of Ford's triumph two disgruntled cycle racers, Barney Oldfield and Tom Cooper, were on hand. They were to have starred in an exhibition with their tandem racer but their efforts were completely overshadowed by Ford's performance. Oldfield grunted something about the automobile being a fad that wouldn't last. Little did they know that in less than two years' time they would be singing a different tune.

As track champion of the United States, Henry Ford had no difficulty in getting financial backing for his proposed automobile manufacturing company and papers were filed on November 23, 1901, for the Henry Ford Company.

Before long, however, friction developed among the stockholders of the new company as the rush was on to build high-priced cars while Henry Ford stuck stubbornly to his idea of a low-priced car for the masses. It did not take matters long to come to a head, and with both sides agreeing that it was impossible to carry on, the company was disbanded.

The scene now changes to the Cow Creek Mine near Montrose, Colorado, where our erstwhile cycle racing team of Barney Oldfield and Tom Cooper had formed a partnership in a coal mine and were planning to become rich mine owners. But after months of back-breaking work the dream faded rapidly and Cooper decided to call it quits. He announced to Oldfield that he was off to Detroit and maybe have Henry Ford build him a racer. The two partners split the thousand-dollar profit from their hard labors and Cooper made his way to Detroit, where he had some money salted away in a bank, while Oldfield returned to professional cycle racing.

Henry Ford continued his experiments and made his third attempt at putting together an organization. Wills was again with him, together with Spider Huff, John Wandersee, and Gus Degner. Tom Cooper had sold Ford on the idea of building two racers but the majority of the financial burden was to be Cooper's. The cars were to be known as Ford-Cooper Specials and their specifications were very interesting.

The integrally cast engine was undoubtedly the largest four-cylinder powerplant ever to be put in a car. Accurately predicting the present-day trend to "square engines," Ford bestowed on his behemoth a seven-inch bore and seven-inch stroke. Its massive piston displacement of 1,080 cubic inches was about four and one-half times that of the modern V-8. In 1902 bigness meant horses under the hood, and Ford let it be known that his machine developed the equivalent of 50 to 75 of them, a most impressive number for 1902.

There were separate exhaust pipes for each cylinder, a practice still followed in racing cars, although nowadays the pipes are not necessarily the same diameter as the exhaust valves. While the exhaust valves rode a cam in the usual manner, the intakes were opened by suction of their respective cylinders. This neat arrangement worked very well, except at high speed, when the intake valves lagged a few strokes behind the pistons.

The crankshaft was optimistically provided with a dirt protector, but aside from this, the rotating parts were exposed to Michigan mud. Attached to the crankshaft was the colossus of all the colossal pieces making up this engine, a 250-pound flywheel, two feet in diameter and half a foot thick. Picture three good-sized manhole covers stuck together and rotating furiously an inch from your shoes, with no floorboards to guard against amputation. Early "hero drivers" really earned their reputations.

A wooden-block clutch expanded against the inside rim of the flywheel, engaging a shaft which drove the rear wheels without benefit of transmission, universal joint, or differential. The red racer had no rear springs. It took Ford many years to be convinced that a rigid suspension system was not necessarily desirable in motorcars, but this was the zenith. The ring and pinion gears which composed the rear end were exposed to whatever mud and dust managed to escape being sucked into the engine. The ratio was a rather unusual 4:5 which combined with the 36-inch rear wheels to produce a kind of super overdrive: 700 rpm propelled the car one mile.

Perhaps it was just as well that the rear end was lubricated with grinding compound, for it is hard to see how any but a set of well-worn, loose-fitting gears could ever survive the punishment meted out by the crowbar-stiff suspension. There is a fable about the immovable object meeting the irresistible force which tells us that despite the adjectives, something has to give. When the red car met an irregularity in the road, it usually took off through the air: the lack of differential action on the rear wheels created a chronic case of skids.

Ford made doubly sure of having a good solid ride by lining the two-by-four white-ash frame with boiler plate. Crossbars of the same composition were liberally added at random. The water supply was located under the driver's seat—undoubtedly one of the reasons why the cooling system underwent three major changes during the car's lifetime. The original radiator, supplied by a gear-driven water pump, consisted of 64 three-quarter-inch brass pipes mounted one above the other; when this was found to be inadequate (mainly because of lack of radiating ribs), more pipes were added until a very Rolls-Royce-like, appearance was achieved. The cooling effect was not Rolls-Royce-like, however, so the beehive structure that is now on the car was installed. This design, plus adequate ventilation, kept the seat and the driver's pants from becoming too hot, and was the radiator used during most of the car's summer weather racing career. In the winter, the remote location of the water tank and the chilly Michigan climate combined to form ice cubes in the cooling system. To solve this problem, Ford provided a cold-weather tank. It was a bullet-shaped affair that sat on top of the engine like a large hood ornament.

The gas tank was mounted on the left of the engine, and was connected by a $2\frac{1}{4}$-inch supply line to that granddaddy of the carburetor, the mixing valve. But there were problems.

The unveiling of the great red Ford-Cooper Special was held in

October, 1902. The first one cost some $5,000 to build, a considerable sum in that day. The story caused quite a stir in the local press. It was mentioned that both Winton's Bullet and Cannon's steamer were already running but that the untried Ford-Cooper Specials would be more than a match for their competitors.

What the enthusiastic writers did not know at the time of writing was that the cars had not run and in fact would not run. Barney Oldfield was setting new records with his cycles in Salt Lake City and the future looked very promising. One day a letter arrived from his ex-partner Tom Cooper that had a marked effect on Barney's future activities.

Cooper explained his association with Henry Ford and asked Barney to join the small group in Detroit as another mechanic was needed. As an added incentive, Cooper mentioned that it was quite possible that Oldfield would get to drive one of the racers. Despite his misgivings about the "new fad," Barney decided to pack his bags and bought a one-way ticket to Detroit. There the association of Ford and Cooper was beginning to come apart. The cars would snort to a start, give a massive lurch and stop again. Henry Ford was unable to solve the problem, and in disgust sold his interest in both racers to Tom Cooper for $350 with the stimulation that the Ford name was not to be associated with the cars.

The problem of starting and keeping the engines running lay with the engine-driven fuel pump being unable to supply enough fuel to fill the enormous 2¼-inch fuel line to the mixing valve. This situation was quickly put right when Barney Oldfield arrived, and using the full power of his bicycle racing lungs he blew into the fuel tank while Cooper operated the crank. The once-reluctant engine burst into life with a roar that shook windows and continued to roar until the lung-pressurized fuel system ran out of breath. It was easy to duplicate this mechanically, and from then on the cars ran perfectly.

Ford got back into the act because his name began cropping up once again in contemporary news articles about the car. Cooper's role was mainly that of the sponsor and he was one of those rare persons who saw to it that credit was given to whom it was due. Henry Ford was welcomed back into the fold and the two men set about solving the problem of how to drive the car, now that the engine was running.

Directional control of a sort was to be accomplished by a type of tiller still seen on steamrollers. A 28-inch horizontal wooden bar was centrally mounted on a vertical post and fitted with a handle at either end. Ford and Cooper found they lacked the strength to successfully negotiate the corners, so both men eyed their mechanic, Barney Oldfield, and his automobile racing career began.

With a minimum of verbal instruction and no practice whatsoever in this or any other car, the young man who had never driven a race before in his life climbed aboard the red racer at the old Grosse Point Blue Ribbon Track, and competing against five other cars, left them in the dust of a world's record 5 miles in 5 minutes and 28 seconds.

Oldfield could have done better had he not continually skidded around the outside of the turns, but at that, he finished a half mile ahead of his nearest rival. Certain people claim that it was at this moment, on December 1, 1902, that Ford really decided to start building automobiles.

During the race, Barney unofficially clocked 1:01.2 for the mile, nosing out Winton's Bullet, which three months before had chugged a measured mile around Cleveland's Glenville track in 1:02.25. Cannon's steam racer was way behind, requiring 1:05.25

to puff the same distance. Cannon was out of the running on another count too, for the recently organized American Automobile Association disqualified the steamer on the ground that two men were required to operate it. This was drawing the line where it hurt, for all contemporary gasoline cars carried "mechanicians," who were absolutely essential if the owner expected to cross the finishing line. Because of the designer's price, not lack of foresight, proper accommodation for these assistant drivers were never provided. They were picked for their jockey-like physique as well as mechanical ability, and had to be untainted by any desire to live to a ripe old age. Oldfield usually carried along Ed "Spider" Huff, a 100-pounder who, while oiling bearings, making adjustments, and otherwise ministering to the needs of the car during the race, clung to whatever surface was available.

Not to be outdone by publicity-conscious competitors, Oldfield dubbed his car 999. A well-chosen title, it was linked with the feats of the record-holding New York Central locomotive, and stuck in the public's mind. Privately, Barney referred to 999 by the generous (but not entirely warranted) nickname of Old Faithful. The machines were raced by Oldfield during the following year and track records were constantly broken.

In August, 1903, the arrangement between Oldfield and Cooper came to an end and Barney signed a contract to drive for Alexander Winton. Cooper engaged Harry Cunningham to drive the 999 and Cooper recovered enough from an appendicitis attack to take on Oldfield in the annual Manufacturer's Challenge Cup race and defeat his former mechanic and teammate. The same month of Cooper's victory, his Arrow was wrecked, killing its driver H. B. Day in a race at Milwaukee. The damaged Arrow was returned to Detroit where it was stored in the yards of the Pere Marquette until the winter, at which time it was completely rebuilt for use by Henry Ford. On January 12, 1904, the rebuilt Arrow reached the apex of its career. On that cold winter morning an automobile not only reached, but (aided by a tailwind) exceeded, 90 mph for the first time in motoring history.

A hundred people or so had gathered on the ice of Lake St. Clair in Anchor Bay, just off the shore of New Baltimore, Michigan. AAA officials had marked off a three-mile straight course, and had scattered cinders in some spots where they considered the ice too slippery for good traction. The timers stood at the beginning and end of the third mile with their checkered flags and stopwatches. Ford and his mechanic, Spider Huff, were down at the other end with 999, getting ready for their two-mile flying start. They worked feverishly with a plumber's torch to warm the cold manifold. Some anonymous hero volunteered to crank, and when the engine caught, the cough of the four great cylinders carried for miles through the crisp air. Spider climbed into position on the frame alongside the engine. His principal duty was to hold the throttle valve wide open, for they had found from experience that the car bounced too much for the driver to keep his foot on the accelerator. Willing hands gave them a push, Ford engaged the clutch, and they were off. All four cylinders worked regularly and the machine, gathering speed, jolted down the course toward the starting line. Every time it hit a bump, all nine feet four inches of car would fly into the air. The two occupants hung on for dear life, and they entered the 15-foot lane in the third mile like an irate Brahman bull. Ford's take-offs and landings had been pretty smooth until he hit a particularly vicious bump along the timed mile. The car took off in a flight that looked like its last, but a snowbank intervened. For a breathless second nothing could be seen but a dense cloud of smoke, steam, and snow. How-

Barney Oldfield at the tiller of the Ford 999 racer. (Ford Motor Co.)

The Ford 999 racer as it is to-day on display at the Henry Ford Museum, Dearborn, Michigan. (Long Island Automotive Museum)

The engine of Ford 999 showing modifications made to the cam gear at a later date. (Long Island Automotive Museum)

ever, somehow Ford and Spider had kept the machine upright and headed in the right direction. They crossed the finishing line, but it was no time to relax: there was nothing but ice and a set of 1902-model mechanical rear-axle brakes between the car and the icebound schooner, *Garibaldi,* dead ahead. The ship loomed larger and larger, and it was obvious that something had to be done.

In keeping with the aeronautical character of the run, Ford made a desperate attempt to spin the car. He succeeded and, when they finally stopped spinning, Ford and Spider, to quote the next morning's Detroit *Tribune,* "looked a bit pale." Men and machine had traveled a mile in 39.4 seconds, a world's record. The same journal remarked: "The kilometer was to be attempted as well, but the danger was so great it was left to the French who invented it."

Cooper still owned both the yellow record-breaker and the red 999. One would think they would have been his most prized possessions, but for some reason obscured by time, two days after the record run, he sold them to an Alabamian named Tom Pickens for an undisclosed sum.

Pickens planned to tour the country with the cars, taking on all comers in races, and generally cash in on the fame achieved by 999. The press of the period was full of Pickens' plans and various other pronouncements of a typical promoter turned publicity man, making it hard to sort fact from fiction. The Arrow was renamed the New 999, while 999 was called Old 999.

He did travel the country extensively with the cars, but bad luck plagued him to the extent that his story reads like Horatio Alger in reverse. Pickens and Old 999 ended up in Salt Lake City on the county fair circuit, both broke—one from lack of money, the other from lack of care.

It had been Pickens' practice to hire the local strongman to drive the car. In Salt Lake City, the crowning blow came when an ex-pug crashed 999 into the guard fence, causing extensive damage to fence, driver, and car. Meanwhile Barney Oldfield had arrived in town; he bought the wreck and sent the Southerner to Los Angeles along with the crated car. The trip must have been invigorating, for Oldfield received a $140 bill for the supposedly prepaid shipment. This was the last straw, and the car went under the railroad auctioneer's hammer.

The car caught the eye of a Californian named Dana Burke, who towed it home to Ocean City. Not much of a handyman, Burke hired Bruno Seibel, a German mechanic who had worked for Daimler Motor Company. However, the rebuilding was never finished. Nostalgic Barney heard of 999's plight and came prepared to repurchase it, but even he was discouraged at the sight of dry rot and twisted, rusty steel, and left empty-handed, to devote full time to his tire business in Los Angeles.

The motoring world and the Edison Institute Museum can thank a San Francisco Ford dealer, William L. Hughson, for rescuing 999 and restoring it to its present fine condition. Hughson's labor was one of love, for by that time faster cars had been built, and like Man o'War, the great red racer was destined to spend the rest of its days watching its progeny eclipse its records but never its fame. Like Man o' War, 999 continued to earn its keep standing on exhibition and helping to sell cars for Hughson until Henry Ford bought it and moved it to Dearborn, Michigan.

Shortly before his death, Ford is said to have remarked to Oldfield: "You made me and I made you." The great Barney shook his head and said: "Old 999 made both of us."

CHAPTER 2

The Model T in Racing

In the years when the Model T Ford became every man's car it was considered a must to own a new one as secondhand ones were regarded as a poor investment because of the tremendous abuse most of them were given.

The resulting low price of used Model T's was the spark that gave budding hot-rodders the tremendous opportunity of acquiring complete machines which could be used and modified without any great outlay of cash and the Model T thus became the training ground for many of America's early auto mechanics.

As always, the young experimenters wanted to extract more performance out of the product and on the simple Model T block began the first nation-wide hot-rod movement.

As the Model T was refined by Ford, one of the steps was to detune it to achieve greater reliability so the budding experimenters reverted to the early production Model T heads which were flatter than the later models. One problem that arose from this modification was that the car was liable to boil with great frequency due to the smaller water passages used in the earlier head. This led to special radiators being offered that had better cooling characteristics and the business of special parts and equipment for racing began.

One of the pioneers of Model T tuning equipment was C. D. Noonan of Paris, Illinois, who advertised an overhead 8-valve unit and was followed shortly after by Craig-Hunt, who announced a 16-valve single-overhead camshaft kit. This early tuning pack came with a straight camshaft and loose cams which were pinned by the experimenter to suit his own tuning needs or his own ideas on valve timing. This was followed by a kit with fixed lobe cams designed for top performance. These early kits worked extremely well and gave excellent performance although they tended to be a little unrealiable. As World War I began, Robert M. Roof offered his 16-valve head, with improvements being incorporated as time passed.

One of the problems with these early head kits was the number of valve failures. Normal Model T cast-iron valves had been used with the idea of cutting down the price, but the cast-iron type proved unsuitable and steel valves soon became available at extra cost. With the success of the Roof head, Robert M. Roof joined a group and formed Laurel Motors Corporation, which manufactured the R. M. Roof kits, although they are frequently referred to as Laurel heads.

The search for lighter parts also began. Green Engineering of Dayton, Ohio, offered aluminite pistons and connecting rods as early as 1915 and went on to produce a large line of speed parts. They also designed a flat head with a more hemispherical head, centered spark plug, and greater cooling area to compete with the more complicated overhead designs.

Morton & Brett were building racing bodies for the Model T

1912 Ford Model T racing engine with a 1923 Waukesha Ricardo head, Winfield carburetor and manifold, Splitdorf magneto, Eskimo water pump, and Centri oiler. (Courtesy of Harrah's Automobile Collection, Reno, Nevada)

1918 Ford Model T racing engine with Roof head (16 valves), Atwater-Kent distributor, Zenith carburetor, Universal water pump, and Faithful oiler. (Courtesy of Harrah's Automobile Collection, Reno, Nevada)

1922 Ford Model T racing engine with Rajo head (8 valves), Delco distributor, Zenith carburetor, Apco water pump, and Faithful oiler. (Courtesy of Harrah's Automobile Collection, Reno, Nevada)

in Indianapolis and Hassler was making underslung suspension parts. More and more people got into the act. There were Rajo heads and Waukesha-Ricardo heads, Champion racing bodies and Craig-Hunt speedway racing bodies, Ruckstell axles special transmissions, and hundreds of other associated parts.

Everywhere the Model T was winning races. Noel Bullock won the Pikes Peak Hill Climb in a much-modified Model T with a Rajo 8-valve head and won 74 races on half-mile and mile tracks in six years with the same car.

Perhaps the most famous name associated with the speed equipment for Fords is Chevrolet. The Chevrolet brothers had been famous for years on the American racing scene as drivers and constructors. Louis Chevrolet's chief engineer, C. W. Van Ranst, suggested that there was money to be made in the field of speed parts for the four-cylinder Fords and further came up with the idea of

1926 Ford Model T racing engine with Rajo head (4 valves), Bosch distributor, Winfield carburetor, Impeller water pump, and Centri oiler. (Courtesy of Harrah's Automobile Collection, Reno, Nevada)

1930 Model A racing engine Miller Schoefield head (8 valves),Wico magneto,Winfield carburetor and manifold. (Courtesy of Harrah's Automobile Collection, Reno, Nevada)

1931 Model A racing engine with Cragar head (8 valves), Wico magneto, Winfield carburetor and manifold. (Courtesy of Harrah's Automobile Collection, Reno, Nevada)

putting together some complete cars and designing their own over-head-valve conversion.

The suggestion fell on receptive ears and work began at the Chevrolet Brothers Manufacturing Company at Indianapolis. For their initial testing they used a Model T which belonged to a shop welder in their employ who used it to haul parts. The deal was that if he lent them the car, they would let him have the modifications free. The results were so good that although he was an experienced racing driver, Chevrolet went so fast that he crashed on the first outing. The damage was not too bad and the car was returned to the welder, Skinny Clemons, who later on became a famous dirt-track driver and car owner.

The Fronty-Ford was born, and after their experience Van Ranst and Chevrolet returned to Indianapolis and immediately com-menced construction of five cars.

The Fronty heads were a tremendous success and production was increased until it topped 60 per day, with more than 10,000 sold before interest in racing Model T's finally ran out.

The Fronty-Fords made their first appearance at Indianapolis in 1922, one being driven by Jack Curtner and the other by Glen Howard. Contemporary reports say that they were completely out-classed, being more suitable for dirt-track racing but nevertheless showed great stamina. Curtner was flagged in fourteenth place and Howard was classified eighteenth after retiring on lap 165 with engine trouble.

It was in 1923 that the future of Indianapolis Motor Speedway was in doubt. The race was marked by the appearance of two Euro-pean teams: Mercedes and Bugatti, the former with Lautenschlager, Wagner, and Seiler as drivers, and the latter represented by De Vizcaya, Cystria, Alzaga, Riganti, and Zborowski. The Barber-

Warnock Ford was entered by the Indianapolis Ford dealership of that name and was built by Louis Chevrolet. L. L. Corum was nominated to drive it, and he qualified at 86.65 mph, most of the qualifiers being in the high 80's and 90's, with the fastest qualifier, Tommy Milton, turning a speed of 108.17 mph.

Tommy Milton won the race that year with his Miller-built H. C. S. Special and Durant Specials, also built by Miller, finishing second and third with Harry Hartz and Jimmy Murphy. The Fronty-Ford put up a consistent performance; Corum drove without a relief driver and made no stops for tires. He averaged 82.58 mph for the 500 miles and left both of the famous European teams behind him to finish a much-applauded fifth.

The success of the one entry in 1923 inspired Barber-Warnock to enter a full team for 1924 and Henry Ford agreed to act as honorary referee for the race.

L. L. Corum finished 5th in the 1923 Indianapolis 500 Mile with a Barber-Warnock-entered Fronty-Ford. (Indianapolis Motor Speedway)

Henry Ford poses in Fred Harder's Barber-Warnock Ford Special at Indianapolis, 1924. Ford was Honorary Referee for the event. Standing behind him are (r. with cigar) Barney Oldfield and (l.) Arthur Chevrolet. (Ford Motor Co.)

The drivers were Bill Hunt in Barber-Warnock Ford No. 26, Fred Harder in No. 27, and Alfred Moss, father of famous British racing driver Stirling Moss, in No. 28.

All three cars had a bore and stroke of 3.115 x 4.0 inches and a displacement of just over 121 cubic inches. One of the cars ran 7:1 compression ratio and had 80 horsepower, while the other two ran 6.75:1 and had 65 horsepower at 3,700 rpm, compared to the 120 brake horsepower of the Miller engines that they were up against. Moss qualified the fastest of the three at 85.27 mph, with Hunt next at 85.04 mph, and Harder at 82.77 mph. This gave Moss and Hunt places on the seventh row of the starting grid and Harder a place in the eighth row.

Fastest qualifier was Jimmy Murphy with a Miller at 108.037 mph and the Barber-Warnock Ford entries were the only cars to qualify at less than 90 mph.

Alfred Moss, father of famous British racing driver Stirling Moss, finished 16th in 1924 with Barber-Warnock Ford Special. (Indianapolis Motor Speedway)

INDIANAPOLIS MOTOR SPEEDWAY ANNUAL 500 MILE RACE 1924
Driver BILL HUNT Car FORD.

Bill Hunt was 14th in the 1924 Indy race in Barber-Warnock Ford Special. (Indianapolis Motor Speedway)

INDIANAPOLIS MOTOR SPEEDWAY
ANNUAL 500 MILE RACE 1924
Driver ALFRED MOSS CAR FORD

The three team cars ran steadily but not impressively throughout the race, having their share of problems. Very early in the race
Bill Hunt's car picked up a piece of paper which clung to the radiator
and began to cause overheating. He came into the pits on lap 12 and
had a quick brake adjustment while the paper was removed. The
whole stop was done in 20 seconds but on lap 22 Hunt was in again.
Oil was leaking from the car and the plugs were fouled, the oil leak
could not be found so the plugs were changed and Hunt was back
in the race after a stop of 3 min. 20 sec. His next stop was for tires,
but in stopping, the driver threw the brake toggles over so far that
both rear brakes seized. In trying to restart the car by pushing, the
dragging brakes made it impossible to push fast enough to start the
engine so work had to be done on the brakes. Both pull rods had to
be straightened and when Hunt restarted he had been in the pits
for 6 min. 17 sec.

A pit signal was given to Alfred Moss to come in for a tire
change. Moss misjudged his speed the first time and was forced to
go around for another lap before pitting. He changed both rear tires,
took on water, and installed a new cap screw in the clutch cover in
2 min. 47 sec.

Fred Harder was the last of the Barber-Warnocks to make a
stop, coming in on lap 53 with an engine misfiring. The spark plugs
were changed and the fuel lines and carburetor cleaned. Water was
added and he rejoined the race after 5 min. 30 sec. Harder was back
in the pits four laps later with a binding carburetor throttle. The
plugs were changed again, the fuel lines and carburetor cleaned out
once more, and the sticking throttle fixed, this time costing him
10 min. 23 sec. The race was won by L. L. Corum and Joe Boyer
driving an 8-cylinder Duesenberg at an average speed of 98.23 mph
and Earl Cooper in a Miller-engined Studebaker was second. Bill

Hunt finished fourteenth, being flagged at lap 191. Alfred Moss, sixteenth, flagged at lap 177, and Fred Harder, seventeenth, also flagged at 177. While the cars ran steadily enough, they were completely outclassed.

The following year, in 1925, a Fronty-Ford was entered as the Skelly Special, with M. C. Jones as driver; it qualified at 88.478 mph, the slowest time of the trials. With most other drivers running 100 mph plus, and Leon Duray fastest at 113.19 mph, the little Ford could hardly expect to be competitive. It was out of the race after 33 laps with transmission failure, being classified twenty-first.

For the 1926 season, Louis Chevrolet built a new Fronty-Ford. It was known as the Hamlin Special and was front-wheel drive. To bring it within the 91-cubic inch limit, the bore and stroke were 2.875 x 3.5 in., achieved by sleeving the stock Ford block and machining a short-throw crankshaft. The engine was installed with

Jack McCarver's Hamlin-Fronty Ford was entered in the 1926 Indy race by the Chevrolet brothers. The car lasted 23 laps before it blew the engine. (Indianapolis Motor Speedway)

its flywheel end forward to match up with the front-wheel drive and at the rear of the engine a Rootes supercharger was gear-driven off the nose of the crankshaft. All critical parts were drilled for pressure lubrication and peak 6,000 rpm was a figure unheard-of for Model T owners. Jack McCarver qualified the Hamlin Special at 86.418 mph for the ninth row, compared to Earl Cooper's fastest speed of 111.73 mph. It was the same story of being outclassed in the big league, and McCarver's run came to an end on lap 22 when a bearing gave out and a connecting rod broke.

However, in the lesser races the Fronty-Fords continued to do well and the Hamlin Special, renamed the Ray Day Piston Special, was still a money-maker in 1932.

In 1930 Chet Miller was entered in a Fronty-Ford by Thomas J. Mulligan and qualified at 97.360 mph, finishing 13th when flagged at lap 161. In 1931 Gene Haustein in a Fronty-Ford entered by

Francis Quinn broke his rear axle after 3 laps in the 1931 Indianapolis race. He drove a Miller chassis fitted with a special Ford Model A engine. (Indianapolis Motor Speedway)

Gene Haustein lost a wheel on lap 117 in the 1931 Indy race. He qualified his Fronty Ford at 108.39 mph. (Indianapolis Motor Speedway)

*Chet Miller's Fronty Ford finished 13th in the 1930 Indianapolis race.
He averaged 97.36 mph. (Indianapolis Motor Speedway)*

Fronty-Ford Sales of Michigan qualified at 108.395 mph and finished twenty-third, losing a wheel on lap 117. It was the end of the road for the 4-cylinder engines and it remained to be seen whether the new Ford V-8's would fare any better.

Frank McGurk retired with a broken crankshaft after lap 51 in the 1936 Indy race. He drove an Adams-chassied Cragar-Ford. (Indianapolis Motor Speedway)

Indianapolis and the Early Ford V-8's

When the Ford V-8 went into production in 1932 it was not long before someone started tinkering with it to produce more power, just as had been the case with the Model T's. The hopped-up Model T's had been enormously successful in track racing but had never been fast enough at Indianapolis, and many hoped that the Ford V-8 would be an inexpensive answer for running in the 500-mile race.

The first such entry was in 1933. C. O. Warnock, who had been associated with the Barber-Warnock Fords, entered Doc Williams in a car named the C. O. Warnock Special. There were many other stock-based racing cars in the 1933 event, with Studebaker having nine entries and Hudson four. As it turned out, the Ford debut was inauspicious, the car was too slow, and Doc Williams failed to qualify. The first of the stock-based racers was the Shafer 8 powered by a Buick 8-cylinder engine, which finished in fifth place.

In 1934 three Ford V-8-engined cars were entered at Indianapolis. Jack Petticord drove the Don Hulbert Ford, Charles Crawford the Detroit Gasket & Manufacturing Ford, and Chet Miller the Bohnalite Ford entered by the Bohn Aluminum and Brass Corporation.

Petticord was unable to qualify his car, Crawford qualified at 108.784 mph, and Miller at 109.252 mph, the latter starting in 32d spot. It was obvious that these cars were outclassed when their times were compared with the 119.329 set by Kelly Petillo on the pole position. Chet Miller's race did not last very long, on lap 11 he jumped the wall at the north bridge, fortunately without injury to himself and his mechanic. Charles Crawford's Detroit Gasket Ford broke a steering knuckle and was towed in. He was allowed to resume the race after fitting a new knuckle but lasted only until lap 110 when a head gasket blew.

Again in 1934 there was a good entry of stock-based racing cars, four Studebakers, two Buicks, two Cummins diesels, one Graham, and one Hudson, along with a DeSoto that was wrecked in practice. Studebaker has gone in for racing in a big way and their advertising has included the slogan "From the speedway comes their stamina, from the skyway comes their style."

Stripped Ford V-8 roadsters driven by Indianapolis drivers completely dominated many of the road races held in 1933 and 1934 and it seemed time for an all-out Ford effort at Indianapolis. This came about through the promotional genius of Preston Tucker (who later also promoted the infamous Tucker rear-engined car), and with a big splash it was announced that a 10-car Ford team was to be entered by none other than famed race car builder Harry Miller.

Four other V-8 Fords were entered, Herb Ardinger with the Welch-Ford, Overton Snell with the Snell Brothers Ford, Doc Wil-

The first Ford V-8 powered car at Indianapolis was driven by Doc Williams in 1933. It failed to qualify. (Indianapolis Motor Speedway)

In 1934 Chet Miller's Bohnalite-Ford V-8 crashed over the southwest wall after eleven laps. (Indianapolis Motor Speedway)

liams with the Harry Henderson-Ford, and Duke Nalon with the Jeeter Morris-Ford. Snell could manage only 99.66 mph and was too slow to qualify; the same happened to Ardinger. Doc Williams' car was wrecked in practice and Nalon's Ford was withdrawn. This left only the Miller-Fords but there was some doubt if all 10 cars would make it on time.

When the first of the Miller-Fords arrived it was impressive in its red-and-cream finish, with a long, low shape with a radiator that resembled the radiator shells of the 1935 Ford passenger cars. The car's arrival had been expected several days earlier and race car production in Miller's Detroit shop was obviously running behind schedule. Miller promised that five more cars would arrive at the speedway before the start of time trials in six days. George Barringer posed with Miller for photographers and then drove a few slow practice laps. Barringer was one of the six drivers nominated for the team at the time of the entry. The others were 1925 race-winner Pete DePaolo, veterans Cliff Bergere, Billy Winn, and Dave Evans. The lone rookie on the team at this time was young West Coast dirt-track star Ted Horn.

Much publicity was made over the fact that the cars were 85 percent stock. However, this percentage applied only to the engines, which were 220.5 cubic inch V-8 blocks. The block, crankshaft, connecting rods, valves, and pushrods were stock. The most radical engine modification was the position of the engine. To facilitate the front-drive unit, the engine had been mounted backward. The rear of the engine, now facing front, was bolted to the aluminum front-drive casting which housed a two-forward and one reverse-speed transmission, ring and pinion gears, and differential. The cylinder heads were made of aluminum and interchanged right with left to place the water outlets at the front of the car.

Ted Horn qualified the Miller-Ford at 113.213 mph in 1935. He was classified 16th after steering seizure on lap 145. (Indianapolis Motor Speedway)

The compression ratio was 9.5:1 and the pistons were of special construction with greater height from head to pin and with four rings. The camshaft was a special grind. The water pump was driven directly by the rear (front) of the crankshaft. The oil pan was enlarged to 2-gallon capacity and its bottom was finned for cooling. A continuous-tube oil cooler was used.

The radiator was of stock construction but differently shaped. A 15-gallon spherical fuel tank with three pointed mountings was used, pressurized by a hand pump located at the right corner of the instrument panel.

A flat, rectangular exhaust pipe made of corrugated sheet metal, 12 inches wide, 1.5 inches deep, and 6 feet long, extended the length of the car and fitted into a depression in the steel floor. There was an air space between the floor and the exhaust pipe. Flexible tubes connected the exhaust manifold to this pipe.

The cars featured independent 4-wheel suspension of cross-lever type with leaf springs. Four quarter-elliptic springs were located at the front and rear. Each spring was fitted with a friction-type shock absorber designed by Miller. The frame side-members were curved on the bottom edge to fit the contour of the body. One cross-member was located at the rear of the engine and two more at the rear of the car, affording a very rigid frame. The cars weighed 1,950 pounds, compared to the stock Ford roadster weight of 2,597 pounds.

The exterior appearance of the cars was very clean. The springs, axles, and brake cables were enclosed by Duralumin arms. The steering linkage was located inside the frame. The steering box was made of aluminum and the gears were bronze. The brakes were stock Ford. The instrument panel included a speedometer reading to 160 mph but not a tachometer. The steering wheel was stock Ford and included the chrome banjo strips. A line from the radiator cap to the rear axle separated the two colors on the two-tone painted cars. At this time many Ford truck fleets were painted in this scheme. On May 14, 1935, there were 34 cars at the track and five more Ford Specials were expected by Saturday. On May 15 DePaolo, Bergere, and Barringer all took turns at the wheel of the single Ford in carburetion tests. One lap was turned at 107 mph.

Rex Mays set the top practice speed of the year with 121 mph on Friday, May 17, and established himself as favorite to win the pole starting spot on the next day. The blue Ford Special to be driven by Dave Evans arrived at the track. That night Bergere quit the Ford team because he considered the cars lacking in both power and speed.

Saturday, May 18, was the first day of qualifications and before sunset, twelve attempts had been made and nine cars were in the starting field. Mays was on the pole at 120.736 mph despite the fact that Kelly Petillo had made the fastest run late in the afternoon at 121.687. Petillo had been disqualified for using five eighths of a pint too much gas in this year of fuel limits. The two Fords made no attempt to qualify on a day highlighted by the seizing of a track ambulance by a spectator for two laps before his ultimate arrest.

Mechanic Jimmy Jackson hauled a third Ford from Detroit and DePaolo quit the team as he considered the cars unready and, as such, unsafe. Sunday was rainy and overcast. The bad weather continued into the afternoon and did not improve until after five o'clock. Mauri Rose qualified the buff-colored FWD Special at 116 mph. Russ Snowberger was the only other qualifier. The fourth Ford V-8 special arrived and Winn practiced in the car reaching a high of 106 mph. Barringer and Evans were also on the track in their Fords.

On Tuesday the weather improved for one of those black days in racing history. Harris Insinger started the proceedings at 9 A.M. by crashing the car entered by Harry Hartz, fortunately without

Johnny Seymour, Miller-Ford, Indianapolis, 1935. Out at lap 71 with a grease leak. (Indianapolis Motor Speedway)

serious injury. At 11 o'clock Johnny Hannon and his riding mechanic Oscar Reeves were out in the Bowes car when Hannon lost control and crashed. Hannon died on the way to the hospital. The day ended just before 5 o'clock with the death of Stubby Stubblefield and his mechanic Leo Whittaker, when the right steering arm broke on the Schafer Buick.

Later in the week speedway management announced that a Ford convertible sedan had been selected to pace the event, with either Edsel Ford or Dearborn Branch Manager Harry Mack as driver. The status of the Ford team was the big question at this time. Five of the ten cars were at the track. The race would be held in one week and not one Ford V-8 Special had attempted to qualify; the cars were bouncing too much on the rough brick surface. Jimmy Jackson wore a football shoulder pad on his left shoulder in many practice rides with Barringer.

Eight Ford V-8 Specials were at the speedway by Friday, May 24. The remaining two cars were scheduled to arrive on Saturday. Rumors concerning the cars were spreading over the huge plant. Some thought that Miller would quit until next year. The hoped-for speed of 116 mph was now lowered to 114 mph. There had been various changes to the unique suspension setup but now all cars were back to the original plan. Horn, Barringer, Winn, and Evans were believed to be ready to qualify the next day. Johnny Seymour stepped into the car vacated by DePaolo; L. L. Corum, Bob Sall, the 1933 Eastern AAA champion, George Bailey, and Wes Craw-ford had joined the team. The most money in lap prizes donated by a single firm came from Ford Motor Company with awards of $100 for 40-, 60-, 105-, 110-, and 180-lap intervals.

Time trials were scheduled from 1 to 7 P.M. on Saturday, May 25. Doc MacKenzie was fast man for the day at 114 mph, the low man in the field was Harry McQuinn, who had qualified at 111 mph. Several of the Fords were on the track, but there was no signal from Miller for a time trial. The cars were seeking more efficient fuel consumption. Fifty thousand fans entered the speedway on Sunday and perhaps the biggest attraction for this largest nonrace day crowd on record was the Miller-Ford team. Could it qualify? "Shorty" Cantlon paced the qualifiers with 118 mph, surpassed only by the front-row California trio of Mays, Gordon, and Floyd Roberts. Shaw was in the field with a high 116 mph run. Again several Fords were on the track, but there were no attempts to qualify them. Three days remained until the 22d annual 500.

Early on Monday afternoon Ted Horn and riding mechanic Bo Huckman pulled away from the pits in the black-and-white Ford V-8 Special and, after a warm-up lap, crossed the start-finishing line to begin the first Ford qualification attempt. The V-8 completed the first lap at 113 mph, a speed which could place the car in the race. The next nine laps were very close in speed and the 10-lap average was 113.213. Horn, Huckman, and the other members of the team were elated. Before the day ended, a second Ford made the field as Johnny Seymour qualified the blue-and-aluminum car at 112.7 mph.

Six positions remained open on Tuesday and seven Fords were ready to try for them and to bump the low qualifier McQuinn from the field; 48 hours remained until the race. Several of the drivers who had joined the Ford team at the end of the month had practiced little. Barringer and Winn, who had been on the track since the arrival of the first car, had not found the combination for a qualifying speed. Time trials began at 9 A.M. due to a threat of rain later in the day. There were stiff crosswinds.

George Bailey qualified another Ford V-8 Special early at 113.432 mph. A shower in the afternoon suspended qualifying.

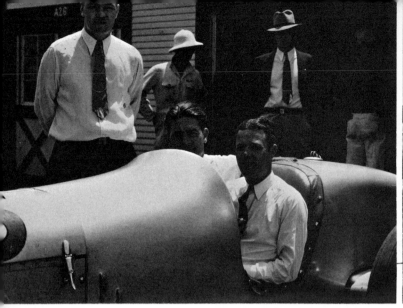

George Bailey, Miller-Ford, Indianapolis, 1935. Out at lap 65 with steering failure. (Indianapolis Motor Speedway)

Bob Sall, Miller-Ford, Indianapolis, 1935. Out at lap 47 with steering failure. (Indianapolis Motor Speedway)

When the track dried, action resumed, and Freddie Winnai, Jimmy Snyder, Harris Insinger, Lou Tomei, and Emil Andres qualified, completing the field. Winn made four laps in the white Ford V-8 Special, but could do no better than 97.5 mph. Barringer completed five laps in the red-and-cream car, which was the first Ford to arrive, but his best lap was only 105 mph.

The 4 P.M. deadline was rapidly approaching. The gold Ford with Bob Sall at the wheel and MacKenzie as mechanic took the green flag and completed 10 laps at 110.5 mph, bumping Andres from the race. Dave Evans was under way at once in the blue Ford, completed 10 laps at 109.9 mph but failed to bump Sall. Evans experienced steering problems on his final laps. Barringer was ready to try once again, but the 4 P.M. deadline passed before Evans completed his run. Crawford in the cream Ford and Corum in the blue-and-white Ford did not attempt to qualify. The tenth Ford was not ready and no driver had been assigned. The field was filled

1935. Dave Evans qualifies his Miller-Ford as first alternate at 109.937 mph. (Ford Motor Co.)

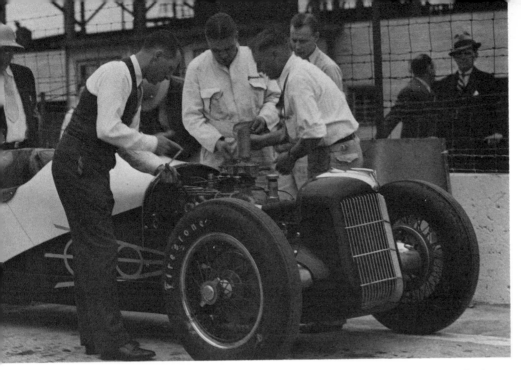

1935. A plug change for the Ford V-8 engine. (Ford Motor Co.)

for the 22d 500 and, for the first time, all cars in the race had qualified in excess of 110 mph.

Thursday, May 30, 1935, was Memorial Day. The band played the national anthem and the largest 500 crowd up to this time stood for "The Star-Spangled Banner." At 9:40 A.M. the official photo was taken and five minutes later the first starting bomb exploded. Bailey's Ford was still being repaired as the one-minute interval bombs began at 9:55. As the cars were being pushed into their starting positions, it was found that Bailey's would not go into gear. This was the fastest of the four Fords in the race and had the famous Art Chevrolet as mechanic.

Horn's black-and-white No. 43 sat ready for action in the middle of the ninth row between the Bowes No. 45 driven by Clay Weatherly and the Ford No. 42 piloted by Seymour. The middle

of the tenth row was held open for Bailey. Poised in 33d and last position was the gold No. 46 driven by Sall.

The Ford convertible sedan driven by Harry Mack with Pop Myers in the front passenger seat pulled away for the pace lap with the crisp bark of the Ford V-8 Specials. The front row of Mays, Gordon, and Roberts followed. Included among the record crowd of spectators were Henry Ford, Edsel Ford, and 2,800 Ford dealers and salesmen from Indiana, Illinois, Ohio, Pennsylvania, and Michigan. The pace lap proceeded down the long backstretch as mechanics worked feverishly to get Bailey's car ready for action. He was going to miss the start and Jimmy Snyder, Harris Insinger, Lou Tomei, and Sall moved up closing the gap.

The Ford pace car dashed down the homestretch and Mack steered to the inside apron as the 10 A.M. starting bomb exploded into the bright Indiana sky. The field, let by Rex Mays, crossed the starting line. Mays streaked into the lead with fourth-place-starter Meyer in hot pursuit. Stapp, Cantlon, Shaw, and Moore were picking up positions as the field completed the first lap and Bailey finally pulled away from the pits to join the race.

Before 10 laps had been completed tragedy struck, Weatherly being killed when he hit the railing.

At lap 10, Rex Mays led Babe Stapp, Lou Meyer, Tony Gulotta, Al Gordon, Floyd Roberts, and Wilbur Shaw. Stapp and Shaw had each gained ten positions in 10 laps. Horn was running 23d, leader of the Ford contingent, Seymour was 25th, Sall 28th, and Bailey 30th. All the Fords had improved upon their starting positions.

At lap 20, Mays was still the leader, followed by Tony Gulotta, Meyer, "Babe" Stapp, Roberts, Deacon Litz, and Shaw. Seymour was now the leader of the Fords holding 20th place at a speed of

100 mph. Mays's speed was 107 mph. Sall was running well; however, at sustained speed the car was overheating and he would have to back off at intervals to permit the car to cool.

At lap 30, Seymour had moved into 18th place, passing Snowberger and Moore; Horn was running behind Snowberger and ahead of George Connor. Bailey, in spite of his late start in the race, was running ahead of Insinger. On lap 47, Sall pitted and was unable to return to the race due to frozen steering gear. One quarter of the race became history at lap 50 as Mays led Stapp and Petillo at 108 mph. Horn held 20th at 102 mph. Seymour came into the pits for 2 min. 45 sec., taking on water and gasoline. Horn was running between Fred Frame and Connor.

At lap 60, Horn was in 18th place following Cliff Bergere in the Shafer Buick. Seymour returned to the pits on lap 61, only 17 minutes after his first stop, due to air pump trouble. George Barringer and Jimmy Jackson replaced Seymour and Kennington in the cockpit and were under way after 20 min. 19 sec. Horn pulled in before Barringer left and took on water and gas. It was a costly stop, taking 3 min. 53 sec.

The Ford pits were very busy as Bailey stopped 2 minutes after Horn had returned to the race, coming in to have his steering checked and oiled. The stop lasted 4 min. 45 sec.; 5 minutes later, on lap 65, Bailey was out for the day. The steering system had frozen—the same problem that had eliminated Sall.

Two minutes after Bailey was officially out of the race, Barringer stopped to have his own steering check and to repair a left rear brake. The steering locked on the blue-and-aluminum car while it sat at the pits and three of the Fords were out after 1 hr., 51 min.

Horn was the only hope of the team. Mays pitted on lap 64 and dropped to fifth place behind Petillo, Shaw, Bill Cummings, and

Ralph Hepburn at lap 70. Horn's long pit stop had dropped him to 21st.

At lap 80, Mays again led as those ahead of his pitted; Horn was 20th. At the next ten-lap interval Mays led Petillo at 109 mph; Horn was 19th at 101 mph. At the halfway mark of 100 laps Petillo had taken the lead from Mays.

Horn was running 16th at lap 120. Four laps later he pitted for water and gas. Again the pit stop was extremely long, lasting 4 min. 45 sec. Still, Horn was 15th by lap 130. Petillo led Shaw, Cummings, Roberts, and Meyer; Mays had dropped out.

At lap 140, Shaw had taken the lead from Petillo and his average speed was 109 mph. Horn pulled into the pits at lap 145, unable to fight the steering wheel for one more lap. He had lasted 3 hr. 41 min., nearly two hours longer than the other Fords.

Petillo regained the lead when Shaw pitted at lap 144. Rain fell from lap 176 through lap 190. Petillo won and, as Shaw took the checkered flag for runner-up spot, the rain began again, bringing on the yellow signals for the remaining finishers.

Time had been the biggest problem faced by Miller. If the project had been started earlier, there would have been time for testing and discovery of the steering-gear weakness. The exhaust manifold was too close to the aluminum steering box and the heat simply caused the bronze gears to expand and seize.

The Miller-Fords ran again at Indianapolis but with the Ford engines replaced by Miller racing engines and in this way they performed a little better.

In 1936 a Ford V-8-engined car was entered under the name of the Lucky Teter Special but was withdrawn.

In the post-World War II period one of the Miller-Fords with a specially reworked Ford V-8 engine was run by the Granatelli

Much-modified Miller-Fords were run post-World War II by the Granatellis. Pete Romcevich drove this Camco Motors Ford in 1947. (Indianapolis Motor Speedway)

1939. Ford V-8 engine with Offenhauser heads and manifold and twin Stromberg "99" carburetors. (Courtesy of Harrah's Automobile Collection, Reno, Nevada)

1938 Ford V-8 engine with Ardun overhead valve heads and manifolds. (Courtesy of Harrah's Automobile Collection, Reno, Nevada)

brothers. In 1946 they entered it as the Grancor V-8 and Danny Kladis qualified it at 118.890 mph, but lasted only 46 laps during the race. In 1947 the car's name was changed to the Camco Motors Ford and Pete Romcevich lasted 168 laps with it, to be qualified 12th in the race. The Granatelli car was later converted to a Mercury engine and appeared again at Indianapolis.

In 1947 there were two other Ford V-8-engined specials entered. Red Byron was down to drive the Pauley Ford and Norm Houser to drive the Robert Allison Ford, but neither progressed beyond the practice sessions.

In 1948 Red Byron was again entered with a Ford V-8-engined car named the Parks-Vogt Special and the Fageol was also Ford-engined. Neither of these Ford-powered cars made the starting lineup, and Ford had to wait until the racing program of the 1960's before the name was again associated with Indianapolis competition.

CHAPTER 4

The Indianapolis Project

Some time after the 1962 Indianapolis 500 race the decision was made to initiate a Ford Indianapolis racing project. The problem of engine design was given to the Advanced Engine Department of Ford's Engine and Foundry Division, which eagerly accepted the task, although there was not much time available to reach the objectives. Hardly any time could be allocated for alternative trials or explorations. The engineers had to adhere to and make the most of whatever key decisions were made along the way.

First of all and most important, the 260 production engine, used in the Fairlane, Falcon, and Comet cars, was selected as most suited to meet readily the Indianapolis displacement limit, which was 4.2 liters or 256.286 cubic inches. A slight reduction in the displacement of the production engine would allow them to meet this race entry regulation.

The use of the 260 engine eliminated the need for the usual

preliminary design which precedes the construction of a new engine. Design did not precede development. Instead, performance data were generated and durability problems raised from existing proto-types. They were studied in the light of sound engineering judgment based on past experience, and submitted to strict computer analysis, which, in coordination with progressive development, produced the final design.

Construction of the chassis was the responsibility of Colin Chapman and his Lotus organization in England. On the basis of Chapman's projected specifications of the car design there was a joint listing of what should be expected from the engine.

The seven objectives were: (1) Complete the race in only one pit stop; (2) carry and consume a total of only 400 pounds of fuel—this precluded the use of exotic fuels involving a penalty of 800 pounds fuel load; (3) carry only 24 pounds of oil instead of the normal 80 pounds; (4) use carburetion in place of fuel injection; (5) limit installed engine weight to 350 pounds; (6) use automotive battery ignition and a distributor instead of a magneto; and (7) develop a minimum of 325 dependable horsepower from 255 cubic inches. A program timing schedule was then set up and this was begun with the decision to make a complete Indianapolis survey in August, 1962.

Investigations of the maximum horsepower capabilities of the Ford production 260 engine were to be completed in September and compared to similar figures obtained from an Offenhauser 4-cylinder Indianapolis engine that Ford had purchased. Vehicle performance tests were to be commenced in October, using a Lotus 25 built for European Formula 1 racing, but having a Coventry Climax engine of known power.

Duplication of the production 260 engine in aluminum and the

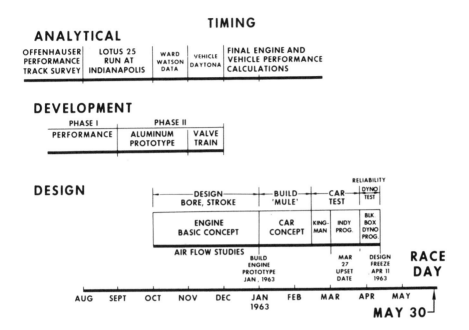

solving of any basic weight or high-speed durability problems was scheduled to be completed by November 1. This month was also the deadline for the assembly of competitive vehicle data to verify the performance calculations and supply analytical results for final engine design and car concept.

All basic engine tests at Daytona Speedway were to be completed before the design freeze on April 11, 1963. As work was under way having the 260 cubic inch engine parts modified, the Indianapolis track survey was also being carried out while yet another team conducted performance tests on the Offenhauser engine on a dynamometer.

The Offenhauser which had been purchased for comparison was a normal 252 cubic inch type with four cylinders and double overhead camshafts. It employed gear train camshaft drive and an exceptionally large induction system designed for fuel injection of methanol and nitromethane. Four valves per cylinder were fitted the bore and stroke of the engine being 4.281 x 4⅜ inches. Compression ratio was 14.95:1 and the whole unit had been tailored to the requirements of the Indianapolis track by camshaft phasing, and the most advantageous locating of its torque peak.

The Ford engineers were quite impressed by the performance of the Offenhauser engine on the dynamometer. It developed 401 brake horsepower at 6,000 rpm and a torque of 378 lb/ft at 5,000 rpm. Since the Offenhauser was calibrated to burn methanol only, the base line was established with this fuel. All data needed for the computer program were extracted from this engine and a complete survey was carried out, including volumetric efficiency, which showed results close to 100 percent for several speeds.

Concurrently the engineers proceeded to run evaluation tests on the modified Ford 260 cubic inch engine. This engine had been modified by the installation of four dual-throat 46-mm Weber carburetors. The intake and exhaust ports and valves were modified on the basis of static bench airflow tests. The combustion chamber was revised by relocating the plug and providing a domed piston with provisions for a three-path flame travel. The resultant compression ratio was 12.5:1. The valve train was revised by adding lightweight mechanical tappets, teflon pushrod guides, dual valve springs, aluminum valve spring retainers, screwed-in rocker arm studs, hollow valves, and a camshaft with a jerk factor of 0.00038 in/deg⁴. The engine easily surpassed the objective of 325 horsepower. But that was on gasoline, and the results were not directly comparable to

PERFORMANCE COMPARISON

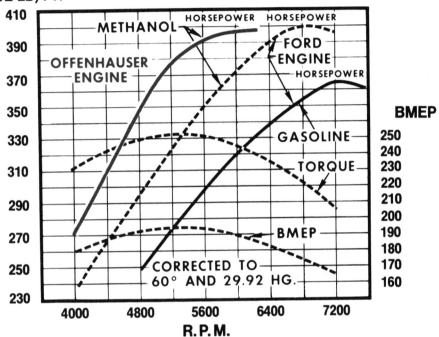

**BRAKE HP &
TORQUE LB/FT.**

R.P.M.

those of the Offenhauser, which was tailored to methanol. This led the engineers into the controversial subject of racing fuels.

The blends of racing fuel that proved best at the time of these tests were aviation gasoline, benzole acetone, methyl alcohol, ethyl alcohol, isopropyl alcohol, and butyl alcohol. Other additive agents such as nitro compounds, water, organic nitrates, peroxides, tetra-ethyl lead, ether, and explosive elements have been used. However, the fuel/air ratio and heating value in Btu/lb are the key to power output. The high specific gravity and the low stoichiometric ratio of exotic fuels presented a disadvantage to the Ford engineers because they wanted to consume only 400 pounds of fuel in the whole course of the race. Ford experimented with several fuels to study their preignition tendencies, octane limit effect, and latent heat of vaporization against volumetric efficiency. Several nitroparaffins were also investigated.

By making several runs on methanol, comparison could be made with the Offenhauser. These data spelled out the distinct advantage of the Offenhauser and substantiated the engineers' previous analytical study. This had indicated that because of the short straightaways, torque wins at Indianapolis.

Data indicated a performance improvement of from 10 to 12 percent by the substitution of methanol for gasoline. Upon adding nitromethane to methanol, data were obtained which manifested an improvement of one third of 1 percent in indicated power for each percent of nitromethane. Consequently, a 20 percent improvement in horsepower was possible with a mixture of 30 percent nitromethane in methanol. This involved a penalty of $2\frac{1}{2}$ to 3 times the gasoline fuel consumption, the question was, "Could the engine tolerate this oxygen-laden fuel?"

Studies of pistons after these tests showed that with the mixture in question, damage was of a high level on the piston crown and skirt and the fuel studies were terminated with the decision to stick to using gasoline as a dependable, low-consumption fuel, and to shun all exotic additives.

Concurrently with the first phase of engine development, the survey of the Indianapolis Speedway was completed. The track is 13,200 feet or 2.5 miles long. The track curves at four 90 degree turns of 1,320 feet separated by two long straightaways of 3,300 feet and two short ones of 660 feet. Its width varies from 50 feet on the straightaways to 60 feet on the turns. Turn banking rises 9 degrees 14 minutes off the horizontal. For "live" interpretation of

FORD LOTUS VEHICLE—INDIANAPOLIS TRACK

MARCH 27, 1963
AVERAGE SPEED 150.501 M.P.H.

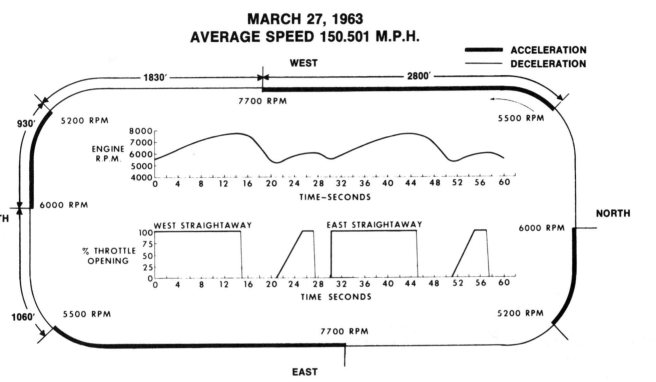

the engineers' track study, Ford enlisted the aid of famous car builder A. J. Watson and equally famous driver Rodger Ward. The Watson and Ward combination had won the Indianapolis 500 in 1959 and 1962. With these two consultants the Ford engineers were able to obtain competitive data on conventional Watson-built cars. One important achievement was the laying out of a complete driving pattern. According to Ward, the normal shutoff point was about two thirds of the way down the long straightaway, at an indicated engine speed of 6,600 rpm.

Engine friction and wind resistance could be depended on to reduce engine speed from a high of 6,600 rpm to 5,200 rpm in the middle of the first 90-degree turn. From this point the engine was accelerated again to 5,600 rpm at the end of the short straightaway, then the resistance dropped the speed to 5,200 rpm in the middle of the second 90-degree turn. At this point acceleration was applied again and the Offenhauser turned 5,600 rpm as it came out of the turn into the back straightaway. These were the elements of a typical lap, and their distribution allowed the engineers to divide the track into four sections. These factors, together with estimating total drag, enabled them to compute vehicle acceleration and deceleration.

The wind resistance for the Watson car was estimated on the basis of a 10.3 square foot frontal area and a drag coefficient of 0.00181. Overall vehicle gross weight was 2,000 pounds, and a drive line efficiency factor of 90 percent was used in the computations. Other data such as tire rolling resistance and previous race speeds of 150 mph enabled the engineers to verify their assumptions when using the output of 400 horsepower from a typical Offenhauser engine.

The data from the Lotus 25 were also used. The Lotus was run with a 1.5-liter Coventry Climax engine of known horsepower, and served to gather drag coefficient data, turn speeds, overall efficiency, and dynamic weight transfer information.

Ford engine performance was substituted in place of that of the Coventry Climax engine to compute the Lotus-Ford acceleration. An assumed gross vehicle weight of 1,600 pounds was taken for the Lotus-Ford, and the drag coefficient was held constant. The frontal area was reduced to 8 square feet. The results of the calculated accelerations indicated that the proposed vehicle would be competitive.

Several speed-time curves were computed, based on average turn speeds from 137.5 to 141 mph, minimum turn speeds of 132.5

mph; but the entering speed increased to 143 mph. In addition, a number of variables were introduced into the computer program in order to develop an ideal driver program from the track data.

Once the desired engine speeds and shutoff points were developed, it became clear that the original objective of 325 horsepower would at best produce an optimum lap speed of only 146 mph; 365 horsepower would produce 150.50 mph; 400 horsepower on methanol would make possible a lap speed of 153 mph; finally, with 425 horsepower on gasoline, 155 mph lap speed could be achieved.

The engineers now had a driver pattern and a horsepower rating that they calculated should run at least 150 mph. This proved to be correct when tests to validate the calculations were held in March, 1963, at Kingman, Arizona, and at the Indianapolis racetrack.

Further work with a Ford engine was required to verify objects not associated with lap speed. A duplicate of the 260 engine, with an aluminum cylinder block and heads, was built for this work. Additional modifications, such as adapting fuel injection, and reducing the displacement to the track regulations, were incorporated. This engine, whether using carburetors with gasoline or fuel injection with methanol, duplicated the power of the originally modified cast-iron production 260 engine.

The lightweight engine was installed in a 1962 Galaxie, and in November the car was shipped to the Daytona Speedway to assess such variables as transient control problems during acceleration, engine crankcase breathing, cooling, starting, battery size, and ignition systems.

Four days and 435 miles of track testing revealed that the fuel injection engine using methanol performed 8.1 mph faster than the carbureted engine using gasoline (154.8 mph versus 146.7 mph, respectively), but this was achieved at a considerable sacrifice in fuel economy, which dropped from 6.41 mpg for gasoline to 2.22 mpg for methanol. Carburetors had been ordered that were larger than the dual-throat Weber type 46 Webers fitted at the time. This modification had the effect of narrowing down the performance difference quite decisively. On this basis, the decision to "go gasoline" was firmly reaffirmed.

Transient condition problems as met in Daytona could not be considered resolved because the high bank angle there (31½ degrees) represented effective G forces substantially lower than for Indianapolis (9 deg. 14 min.). On the other hand, all crankcase breathing and cooling problems were resolved, and generator and battery sizes were selected. Ignition problems were solved by the use of a special transistorized system of a breakerless type, based on a variable reluctance principle. This design employed a concentric permanent magnet and coil with toothed rotor which varied the reluctance of the magnetic circuit as it rotated and thereby generated a voltage wave form in the coil. It was decided for reliability reasons to operate at a fixed timing of 51 degrees before top dead center at 1,000 rpm. As previously mentioned, the combustion chamber was modified for a three-path flame front for best breathing performance. This combustion chamber design required a high spark advance and thereby caused a starting problem in the car at Daytona. The problem was solved by retarding the spark timing 30 degrees during the cranking cycle, by means of a switch positioned between the distributor and amplifier. This switch momentarily reversed the output from the magnetic circuit and the result was approximately 20 degrees spark advance during engine cranking.

Two problems that were indicated on dynamometer tests were confirmed on the aluminum engine during the vehicle tests. Valve train limitations and head gasket problems were encountered as the car moved into higher speeds. The gasket problem was solved by separating the cylinder head from the block with an air gap of approximately 0.012 and using a mechanical joint for sealing. Rubber "O" rings transferred the water through the dry head deck from the cylinder block to the cylinder head. An interesting aspect of this design was that in case a cylinder head joint failed at high speeds and the resulting leakage rate be no greater than the piston ring gap, the failure did not affect horsepower and vehicle performance. The analytical study of high-speed valve train problems involved programming the Indianapolis track cycle and the program was not finalized until March, 1963.

DESIGN APPROACH

Ford's approach to this effort was unusual in that development preceded design. Information drawn from the development program and analytical studies affected the design approach. Various racing engines were compared to the modified Ford cast-iron and aluminum engines and conclusions were drawn that piston acceleration, not piston speed, limited an engine's performance. Accelerations much in excess of 100,000 ft/sec^2 produced inertia forces on all reciprocating parts which in turn limited the peaking speed of a given engine design. The Offenhauser reaches this limit at 6,200 rpm and the Coventry Climax at 6,800 rpm.

The Hepworth and Grandage formula for maximum piston acceleration was then applied to the Ford engine to help establish a bore and stroke that would command the highest peaking speed. The formula gave the Ford engineers a clue as to why Offenhauser engine builders considered rod center distance and rod angles as prime factors for maximum performance.

The Ford engine. (Indianapolis Motor Speedway)

A saying has it that revolutions are of an abstract nature. They cost nothing, weigh nothing, and have neither shape nor substance. Ford's analysis disproved the idea that increasing the revolutions always increases the benefit derived from the engine, and also the idea that the one who can make the engine revolve fastest, while it stays in one piece, will necessarily obtain the highest horsepower.

The formula left open another controversial subject as to what the relation between bore and stroke should be, even in the case where displacement was limited to 4.2 liters (256.284 cu. in.). Strict applications of the piston acceleration theory dictated that stroke. This in turn allowed for a large bore and considerable valve area per square inch of piston. The drawback was that an extra large bore would work adversely on the compression ratio.

Various bore sizes were studied, together with the various valve arrangements, set up for the maximum compression ratio obtainable with the type of camshaft being considered. These different shapes of chambers and valve arrangements were evaluated for both a pushrod engine and the possibilities of going on to a double overhead cam.

Various sizes of straight valve versus bore sizes were compared. As a follow-on step, the valves were canted 7 degrees to form a compound valve angle. A pent chamber with four valves per cylinder and horizontal inlet ports was evaluated and a pent chamber with a vertical inlet port was also examined.

At the conclusion of the studies the engineers arrived at a bore size of a 3.76 inches, only 0.04 inch at variance with the Ford 260 production engine, and the stroke remained the same, at 2.87 inches.

DESIGN COMPONENTS

Based on the analytical and development program, design modifications affecting practically every component were required in order to achieve more than twice the power of the original engine, with 25 percent less weight. In spite of these modifications the Indianapolis engine of 1963 retained a remarkable degree of resemblance to the production engine. The design modifications of the major engine components were: (1) Bore size was reduced from 3.80 inches to 3.76 inches to give a 255 cubic inch displacement; (2) front flange was modified to receive cases for gear-driven camshaft, water pump, distributor and oil pumps; (3) deck thickness was increased 50 percent, to .640 inch; (4) bolt bosses were made longer, to obtain a minimum of two times the diameter thread engagement; (5) main bearing cap mounting face was extended to accommodate 4-bolt nodular iron bearing caps; (6) modification of the head face permitted the use of two additional studs per cylinder; (7) provisions were made for installing dry cast-iron liners with a light (0.001 in.

to 0.002 in.) press fit; (8) in order to seal the combustion gases, a groove was provided in the liner flange for a metal "O" ring gasket which consisted of five laminated steel discs in a flanged steel casing resembling an "O" ring; and (9) with cylinder head and block faces sealed, allowance was made for two oil drain-back holes and one oil pressure hole at the front, also two water transfer holes and one oil drain-back hole at the rear. These holes were sealed with conventional rubber "O" rings. The "O" ring around each cylinder bore the whole concentrated load from the cylinder head studs, and a 0.010 to 0.015 inch air gap was created between the faces of the cylinder block and head.

The cylinder heads, like the block, were made of sand-cast aluminum, from reworked experimental 260 engine patterns. They featured: (1) aluminum bronze valve guides, hardened steel valve seat inserts, and steel valve spring seats; (2) revised water jackets which redirected the water outlet from the intake manifold face to the front of the head, and an added boss to supply pressure oil to the overhead valve train; (3) four bosses added to the outboard (exhaust manifold) side, and four studs added on the intake side of the cylinders to improve gasket sealing; and (4) enlarged intake and exhaust ports, with modification of the combustion chamber.

The crankshaft was made of 4136 steel with revised counterweighting. For space considerations, a #5 counterweight was added to the shaft to eliminate the need for external balance. Rod and crank pins were cross-drilled to meet the needs of high-speed lubrication. To reduce counterweighting requirements, the pins were drilled from both ends and plugged with steel cap plugs, backed with swaged steel pins. The crankshaft damper featured a redesigned inertia member with increased rubber contact area and an added fail-safe lip to prevent dissociation if the rubber bond failed in service.

The pistons were impact forged from high silicon aluminum alloy, they had domed heads with valve clearance pockets and a specially shaped deflector to provide a 12.5:1 compression ratio. The diametric clearance between the piston and the bore was 0.012 to 0.014 inch, with no cam drop. The pistons carried two chrome-faced 1/16-inch-wide compression rings and one 1/8 inch width oil control ring.

The connecting rods were shot peened and polished to remove surface stress raisers; also, the oil squirt holes were eliminated. Larger diameter cap bolts were incorporated to withstand the increased inertia loading generated by the higher operating speeds. A bronze bushing was incorporated to accommodate the free-floating piston pin design.

The increased lubrication needs of the engine were met by an enlarged lubrication system operated by a pressure pump and a scavenge pump. The pressure pump, mounted on an extension of the front main cap, pumped oil from an external tank, and supplied pressure through the number one bearing cap into the block gallery system. The scavenge pump had a 50 percent greater capacity and was mounted on an extension of the number two main cap; it picked up return oil from a baffled cast-magnesium pan, pumped it through a fitting in the front cover back to an external oil tank. The pressure pump was driven by a gear through a tube fitting in the front cover, at 0.727 crankshaft speed. The scavenge pump was powered by an extension of the front pump shaft.

The oil pan was of cast magnesium with internal bolt bosses to mount a steel windage baffle. External bosses at the rear provided for engine assembly hookup to the chassis, and for supporting the transaxle unit.

The magnesium front cover housed the gear train and accommodated drives for the distributor, tachometer, and fuel pump above the crankshaft seal. A large opening piloted the water pump assembly. In addition to the oil scavenge outlet and oil pressure pump inlet tube connections, the front cover provided for piloting and mounting the gear-driven generator, it also supported the engine assembly through mounting bosses added to each side.

The water pump assembly consisted of an aluminum housing, a sealed bearing with extended shaft, a 3⅜-inch diameter cast-iron impeller, and a steel cover plate. It was driven at 0.727 crankshaft speed, with the water from the inlet being routed internally to the rear of the housing, through the impeller, to the outlets located on each side, then out through steel tubes into each bank of the cylinder block to the two outlet holes at the rear of the engine, where it was directed into the cylinder head. The water left through one-inch diameter outlets located in the front of each head, then entered a deaerating unit, and was finally piped to the radiator.

Other parts that required special attention were the valve train arrangement and the intake manifold. The extremely high valve lift and camshaft design required for maximum performance caused orbiting of the rocker studs and lubrication problems at high speeds. Component weight was reduced through tappet redesign, and the sprung weight of the pushrod and tappet was removed from the system. The lubrication problem was minimized by reducing unit pressure by the use of a simulated rocker shaft mounted on a lock stud.

In general, the engineers concluded that the problem with a pushrod engine centered on the pushrod itself. The objective of 8,000 rpm could be obtained only with a large pushrod diameter. The maximum valve lift was 0.51 and the jerk factor of the camshaft was 0.00038. This amount of valve lift was dictated by the port air flow studies, and a total spring force of 450 pounds was required at valve-open position. It was necessary to increase the camshaft post diameter between the lobes, and to employ a helper spring to minimize the weight of the tappet and pushrod. A 7/16-inch diameter pushrod with welded-end construction was required, based on deflection studies. An SAE 6,150 vacuum arc-melted steel was used for the valve springs. The operating stress was 150,000 psi.

A cast rocker arm was used, incorporating a jam nut and locking tab to prevent the adjusting screw from working loose due to high speed vibrations.

The selection of the final gear drive and valve train arrangement was made after a comprehensive analytical study. This information, added to the evaluation of experimental valve train components made on the 260 engine, indicated that a rocker shaft design was more suitable for the aluminum engine.

The induction system included specially designed dual-throat 58 mm downdraft Weber carburetors. These combined separate idling and main systems, the latter discharging in the center of a long boost venturi. Idle transfer was accomplished by three holes approximately 12 degrees from the closed plate position.

The intake manifold featured short direct ports from the carburetor to the cylinder head, and a ribbed mounting flange to minimize throttle plate deflection. This was a simple green sand casting as the engineers anticipated the need for flexibility in carburetor positioning and the possibility of a changeover to 54 mm or 48 mm Webers, based on exhaust system development.

The final determination of the intake and exhaust system and approval of the 58 mm carburetors were reached during the Kingman, Arizona, and Indianapolis trial runs. The exhaust system arrangement was selected from seven systems tested. It consisted

Lotus-Ford on the chassis dynamometer with the early type exhaust system. (Ford Motor Co.)

Rear of Lotus-Ford chassis showing unequal length drive shafts. (Indianapolis Motor Speedway)

The reserve car, called the mule, with early style exhausts. (Indianapolis Motor Speedway)

of equal-length (31.7 in.) exhaust piping arched and crossed over toward the rear of the engine and terminating in two main diffuser assemblies. The exhaust pulse was equally spaced between the collectors at 180 degrees between the cylinders, and scavenging was aided by a divergent trumpeting section. The other systems were discarded on the basis of chassis testing at Kingman and Indianapolis, and wind tunnel testing at Dearborn. Each system presented some advantages, but the engineers considered such items as wind resistance on the vehicle running at 180 mph, and driver's vision, as the two factors for their selection. Added to these were the effect on acceleration, peak performance, and area under the torque curve from 5,500 to 7,500 rpm.

The exhaust system was not the main reason for the tests of the car at Kingman and Indianapolis. The concept car, referred to as the "mule," was scheduled for shakedown testing and application

The Ford engine installed in Dan Gurney's chassis. (Indianapolis Motor Speedway)

engineering, with emphasis on vehicle systems. Such car variables as cooling, fuel, induction, and lube oil were evaluated. The main purpose of the test was to develop programming data for the dynamometer reliability testing program. Sixteen parameters which included engine revolutions per minute and throttle angle were measured. The oscillograph instrumentation installed in the "black box" at the rear of the vehicle provided an accurate record. At the beginning of the analytical studies, lap speeds were computed simulated for a vehicle at Indianapolis on the basis of the vehicle's ability to accelerate at various rates from 137 mph to 180 mph. The Kingman test track was laid out to simulate the equivalent of one turn and one straightaway at Indianapolis. This permitted the programming and setting up the vehicle for the projected 150 mph speeds at Indianapolis. The data from these tests were analyzed and it was concluded that the analytical study had been correct: the car should in fact be capable of laps of 150.50 at Indianapolis.

The reserve Lotus-Ford with and without body shows snug driver's fit. (Ford Motor Co.)

The Lotus-Ford stripped of body, showing upper fuel tank location. (Robert P. Tronolone)

From Kingman, Arizona, the car was immediately shipped to Indianapolis where a systems analysis was again conducted on March 27, and the black box data was validated at the speedway. The official lap speed on the last day of testing at the Indianapolis Speedway was 150.501.

All data were reviewed and the Ford engineers determined that they had a competitive vehicle. All further work, at that time, on the double overhead camshaft engine for the 1963 race was discontinued and in view of the results, Lotus proceeded with the construction of the two rear-engined race cars.

The Lotus was of monocoque construction and carried 46 gallons of gasoline for the Indy 500 in six separate fuel tanks interconnected with special nonreturn valves. This special design feature helped equalize the tire wear on the two Lotus-Fords by preventing the gasoline from surging into the right-hand tanks when the cars entered a left turn.

The Lotus-Fords used two oil tanks. The main tank carried 15 quarts of engine oil. The second, of one-gallon capacity, was used exclusively for the four-speed Colotti gearbox. The oval radiator combined both oil- and water-cooling sections. For the Indianapolis race, the overall length of the Lotus was increased by 5 inches to 150 inches—partly to accommodate 6 foot 2 inch driver Dan Gurney's long legs. Other figures were: Wheelbase 96 inches; body width 28 inches—65 inches between the wheel rims; overall body height, 30.5 inches. To reduce weight transfer under cornering, the chassis was offset $2\frac{3}{8}$ inches to the left of the center line of the car's track. The offset added no greater stability to the vehicle in the turns, but greatly reduced tire wear caused by weight transfer in the four left-hand Indianapolis track turns.

To accomplish the chassis offset, the front suspension links were made longer on the right side. The rear suspension links were of equal length and the chassis merely offset on them. The front suspension was by means of unequal length wishbones giving 2-inch roll center, the cantilever top wishbone operated inboard mounted a coaxial coil Armstrong spring/damper unit and an antiroll bar.

At the rear unequal length track control arms were used giving 2-inch roll center together with a triangulated lower wishbone operating outboard mounted coaxial Armstrong coil spring/damper units with parallel tracking arms and an antiroll bar. The normal rubber drive-shaft couplings, of sufficient size to cope with the torque delivered by the Ford engine, were too large to be incorporated within the body contours, and sliding spline shafts were found to have a tendency to lock up. Consequently, Saginaw recirculating ball splines with normal joints at either end were used in the Lotus-Ford Indianapolis car.

The Lotus-Ford was fitted with Girling $10\frac{1}{2}$-inch disc brakes all round, with provisions for mounting brakes of larger size in case these should be needed. The front and rear hubs were designed to accept peg drive, knock-off, wide-rim wheels of either 15-inch or 16-inch diameter. These special wheels were manufactured specifically for the Lotus-Ford by Dunlop. The Dunlop tires fitted were 16×5.50 or 15×6.0 at the front and 16×7.0 or 15×8.25 at the rear. Steering was by rack and pinion with a three-spoke light alloy steering wheel with $2\frac{1}{4}$ turns from lock to lock.

Further vehicle development continued on a modified Galaxie because the Lotus-Ford indicated a carburetor calibration deficiency at part throttle during trial runs at Indianapolis. G forces of 1.3 in the horizontal and approximately 1 in the vertical could not be duplicated on the dynamometer. Consequently, a Galaxie chassis was employed for testing at the Dearborn Test Track. Using the

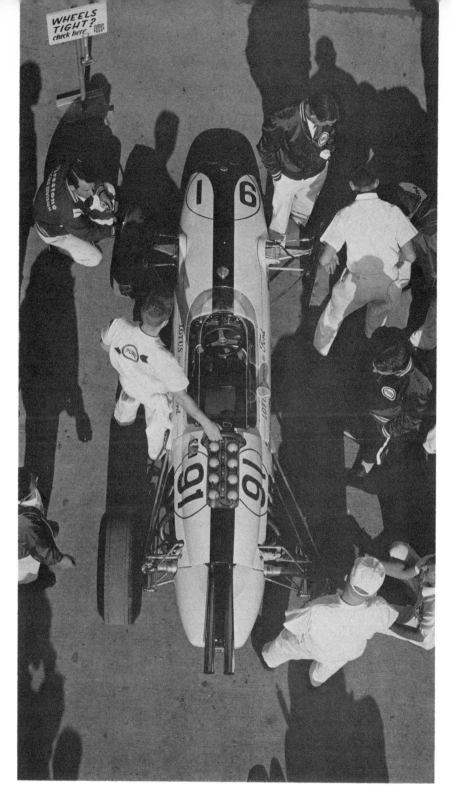

Dan Gurney's Lotus-Ford. (Indianapolis Motor Speedway)

Ford engine being uncrated.
(Indianapolis Motor Speedway)

Indianapolis carburetor calibrations and exhaust system, the engineers studied the eight single cylinders (the intake manifold did not contain a balance tube or plenum) and modified the carburetors and accelerator pump calibration on the vehicle and carburetor flow box. The same Galaxie vehicle, with the body removed, was set up in a wind tunnel so that environmental conditions could be factored into the final manifold, exhaust system, and carburetor calibration.

The engine from the Indianapolis tests, which had run 457 miles, was placed on a dynamometer, durability, and reliability program. A dynamometer test procedure was developed as the result of programming the data of the black box instrumentation on the mule car. Dynamometer testing followed three basic steps. The first one was a 45-minute high performance break in, to perform preliminary checks and provide an initial period of friction reduction. The second step consisted of full-throttle installed engine performance from 2,800 rpm to 8,000 rpm. The third step was a 5-hour Indianapolis high speed cycling durability schedule. Starting at 5,500 rpm, the engine was then accelerated to 7,700 rpm in 15 seconds. In accordance with the black box, the throttle was closed and the engine decelerated to 5,200 rpm in 6 seconds. The throttle was opened at a controlled rate until the engine accelerated to 6,000 rpm in 6 seconds. Following this, the throttle was closed and engine decel-erated to 5,500 rpm in 3 seconds. This sequence lasted 30 seconds, equivalent to half a lap at Indianapolis. It was repeated a total of 600 times, with allowance for three periods of idling at 1,500 rpm, and no lead for 1 minute at 1 hour and 15-minute intervals to simu-late a pit stop. Once this procedure ended, the engine was removed from the dynamometer cell, completely dismantled and inspected.

Based on the reliability testing, the order to freeze the design was given on April 11, 1963, with the following intra-company communication:

Subject: *Engine Design Freeze*

Our examination of the final special high performance 255 cu. in. engine running at the Indianapolis Track and on programmed Indianapolis dynamometer cycle has indicated to all of us that there are no basic engine problems.

Therefore, the AX-230-2 engine design level is hereby frozen. It is fully recognized that no engine is ever completely devel-oped, and improvements can always be made in performance, durability, reliability, and fuel economy. However, this policy, and the deferment of the overhead cam engine, have been im-plemented to eliminate the possibility of a minor design change which could result in post race day hindsight.

W. H. GAY, *Product Engineering Office, Engine and Foun-dry Division, Ford Motor Company.*

For the Indianapolis race the drivers contracted were World Champion Jim Clark and Dan Gurney. There was some controversy

Jim Clark, Lotus-Ford Indianapolis, 1963. (Indianapolis Motor Speedway)

whether the 15-inch tires used by the Lotus-Ford team did not give it a certain advantage and the drivers of the Offy roadsters all demanded 15-inch tires from the manufacturers.

Clark first had to pass his "rookie" test before he could make any high-speed runs at the Indianapolis track. He completed his final phase of runs on May 4. The next day Clark made the first attempt at running at speed. The conditions were windy and overcast, not the ideal situation for best performance. For several laps the Lotus-Ford ran with Bobby Marshman's Offy roadster turning speeds of 148 mph, the Lotus-Ford getting the better of the duel. However, Colin Chapman expected to get better performance from the car as a representative from the Weber factory was on his way from Italy to tune the carburetors.

On May 6 Gurney was out and set the fastest lap at 149.975 mph, being a fraction off the official record. Clark backed him up

Jim Clark practices refueling. (Indianapolis Motor Speedway)

Colin Chapman, designer of the Lotus, consults with Jim Clark. (John W. Posey)

Dan Gurney, Lotus-Ford Indianapolis, 1963. (Indianapolis Motor Speedway)

with a speed of 149.303 mph. The fastest Offy roadster was that of Jim McElreath with a speed of 149.4 mph. After the day's stint Clark and Gurney left for Europe as they had commitments on the Grand Prix circuit.

With the two Lotus-Ford drivers in Europe, Parnelli Jones set the pace with his roadster, and fitting a set of 15-inch tires turned a speed of 152.027 mph, with the roadsters of McElreath and Marshman following with speeds of 150 and 149.8 mph, respectively.

On May 13 Jim Clark was back, fresh from his victory in the British Grand Prix. During the day he clocked the fastest speed with a lap at 149.7 mph. By May 15 Clark was over the 150-mph mark; however, Parnelli Jones was running steadily over 150 with one lap at 153.1 mph.

The big day was May 18 as the cars began to line up for qualification. During early-morning prequalification practice the

Gurney looks pensive as he is about to attempt qualification. (Indianapolis Motor Speedway)

While trying to qualify, Gurney crashed.

Lotus-Ford team suffered an unfortunate blow when Dan Gurney crashed into the wall on the southwest turn and damaged the car so badly he had to transfer to the third Lotus-Ford, the mule, for his qualification attempt.

Some 200,000 spectators watched the start of qualifications and pole position went to Parnelli Jones at 151.153 mph. In second place sat the supercharged Novi of Jim Hurtubise with a speed of 150.257 mph, and in third was Don Branson with an Offy roadster at 150.188 mph. Jim Clark qualified the Lotus-Ford for fifth spot at 149.75 mph and thus started in the middle of the second row between Rodger Ward and Jim McElreath.

Gurney attempted to qualify late in the day but on lap 4, after three laps at 149-plus mph, his foot became entangled in the throttle strap and he was forced to wave off. As Gurney's run had begun just 22 seconds before the 6 P.M. gun ending qualification for the

Jim Clark qualifies at 149.750 mph. (Robert P. Tronolone)

Cockpit layout of Gurney's Lotus-Ford. (Indianapolis Motor Speedway)

Benson Ford poses with Gurney's car before the start of the race. (Indianapolis Motor Speedway)

day, there was no chance to make another attempt. Gurney finally qualified with a speed of 149.019 mph, giving him a position in the fourth row next to Chuck Hulse and Eddie Sachs.

On race day the weather was fair and clear with a slight wind blowing. As the pace car pulled off and the green flag fell, Clark immediately moved up but it was the screaming Novi of Hurtubise that dived toward the inside of the first turn. With Clark and Gurney playing it safe, it was the Novi first, with Parnelli Jones

The parade lap, Clark in 6th position. (Indianapolis Motor Speedway)

Lap 1, the Lotus-Fords are 8th and 9th. (Indianapolis Motor Speedway)

second, and A. J. Foyt third as lap 1 was completed. Jones took over the lead from Hurtubise on lap 2 and began to set a blistering pace while Clark and Gurney contented themselves with lying back and averaging a steady 147 mph.

After 24 minutes of racing Jones had a lead of 8 seconds and the two Lotus-Fords maintained position in the lead pack. The speed picked up as Jones was turning 150-mph laps but would have to

Gurney leads Clark. (Dave Friedman)

make more than one pit stop while the two cars of Clark and Gurney counted on making only one. By 11:45 Clark had passed his teammate Gurney and the two Lotus-Fords were in eighth and ninth places, and at 12:05, as some of the cars began to pit, the Lotus-Fords began to move up.

On lap 64 Parnelli Jones had to pit and Jim Clark made his move, picking up two cars coming down the front straight. Jones was in the pit for only 21 seconds but long enough to allow the two Lotus-Fords to move up rapidly. Clark swept by Sachs into third place and on lap 67 into first, with Gurney in second.

Jim Clark. (Robert P. Tronolone)

Special jacks were used for **81** the Lotus-Ford pit stops. (Indianapolis Motor Speedway)

As Gurney pulls out of the pits, Clark goes by in the lead. (Indianapolis Motor Speedway)

Parnelli Jones put on as much pressure as he could to regain his lead, and by 12:18 he was back in third place, 18 seconds behind Clark and Gurney, who were 5 seconds apart. Jones was catching Clark at the rate of 0.5 seconds per lap. At 12:35 Jones was only 8 seconds behind Clark and Dan Gurney headed for the pits. The stop was slow as the car did not have built-in jacks and had to be maneuvered onto a platform.

At 12:39 Jim Clark pitted and Parnelli Jones retook the lead. The pit stop lost Clark too much time, and by 12:55 Jones had a lead of 48 seconds over the Scotsman. Clark turned several laps at 149.9 and began to gain on Jones, but by 1:30 the Jones roadster had a lead of 42 seconds. A. J. Foyt with another roadster was third, and Gurney held down fourth with the second Lotus-Ford.

Dan Gurney. (Robert P. Tronolone)

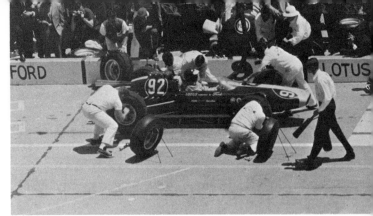

Sequence of Jim Clark's pit stop. (Indianapolis Motor Speedway)

Ready to go.

Clark about to lap Ebb Rose. (Robert P. Tronolone)

When the yellow light went on, Jones took the opportunity to make another pit stop, and as a result Clark moved up to within 11 seconds of the leader; at the same time Gurney got ahead of Foyt to secure third place. By 1:55 Jones was running as fast as he could, turning laps of 151 mph, but Clark was keeping pace. By 2:00 Clark had the Lotus-Ford to within 8 seconds of the roadster and then the yellow was on again after Eddie Sachs spun.

Clark laps McElreath. (Dave Friedman)

Immediately afterward it was noticed that Clark was dropping back a little and a big argument developed in the pits that Jones should be black-flagged as there was oil smoke coming from the exhaust and streaks of oil covered the tail of the car. The yellow went on again when Eddie Sachs lost a wheel and this time Clark lost more time under the slippery conditions and fell 21 seconds behind Jones with seven laps to go. Jones was not black-flagged and at 2:29 the checkered flag was out for the roadster, with the Lotus-Ford finishing in second place.

There was a great deal of discussion about the oil situation after the race, but the important point was that the two Lotus-Fords had run like clockwork and finished in second and seventh places first time out.

CHAPTER **5**

The Twin Cam Engine

The great success of the 1963 Indianapolis project was the main reason behind the decision to make major design revisions for the 1964 event. The Ford engineers felt that the 1963 Lotus-Ford combination had adequately demonstrated the advantages of the new layout and that it was certain a considerable number of race car designers would incorporate the Ford-Lotus concept in their own design ideas. The result of this would naturally be more competitive opposition, and if Ford was to remain ahead it would require a car of significantly higher performance potential.

The 1963 pushrod engine had delivered close to its ultimate capacity in achieving 375 horsepower from its 255 cubic inch displacement and 360 pounds of weight; it appeared obvious that a design change was needed to be competitive. After an analysis of the competitive experiences of 1963, the engineers established a series of objectives for the 1964 engine: (1) Make the Indianapolis 1964

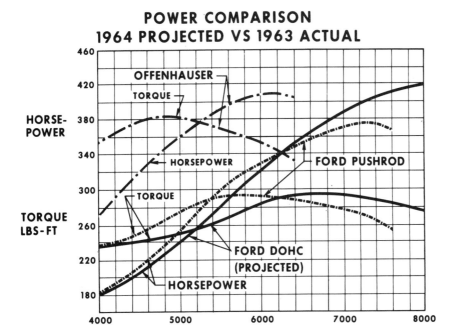

POWER COMPARISON
1964 PROJECTED VS 1963 ACTUAL

version of the Fairlane engine as competitive horsepower-wise as possible, at the minimum feasible revolutions per minute; (2) hold the total engine weight to 400 pounds; (3) utilize gasoline, and thus maintain stock-car image; (4) retain carburetors, if possible, or adopt some known fuel injection system.

These four objectives were not that easy to achieve, the first one alone implying an increase in horsepower in the order of 50, or about 13 percent. The 1963 figure of about 375 brake horsepower would have to be raised to approximately 420 or 425 within the 255 cubic inch displacement limitation of the Indianapolis race. The second objective was no less easy as, in effect, it required that the increased performance be obtained with only 11 percent increase in weight over the 1963 figure of 360 pounds. The third and fourth objectives did not in any way lessen the task, and a better appreciation of the problem can be gained from the power comparisons in the accompanying diagram.

Once the program objectives had been established, the engineers then undertook an analysis of the design implications and the formulation of a plan of action for the design, development, and fabrication of both experimental and race engines. Among the first criteria revealed by the analysis was the establishment of 8,000 rpm as the approximate level necessary to achieve the horsepower objective.

Valve gear and induction system limitations of the pushrod design clearly indicated the need for a double overhead cam configuration, and it was necessary to defer consideration of the other objectives until the design, building, and testing of the first experimental overhead camshaft engines had been completed.

At this point it was decided to lay out a three-phase develop-

The experimental Ford Phase I engine. (Ford Motor Co.)

ment plan for the total program. Phase I would involve the design, fabrication, and evaluation of a double overhead camshaft engine that would utilize as many as possible of the basic components of the 1963 pushrod engine. Phase II would provide for a new series of experimental engines, incorporating design changes resulting from analysis of Phase I test results, with special attention to combustion chamber configuration, induction system design, and to multiple ignition points in the combustion chamber. Phase III would be essentially the Indianapolis race engine, incorporating all design

The gear drive of the Ford double overhead camshaft engine. (Ford Motor Co.)

changes validated by the tests and evaluations resulting from Phases
I and II. Testing during Phase III would result in incorporation of
design refinements of the final engines, right up to race day.

The program began by building an engine, using the cylinder
block, crankshaft, connecting rods, bearings, water pump, oil pumps,
alternator, oil pan, and component gear drives of the 1963 engine.

The purpose of the first experimental engine was to provide
the factual basis for (1) the determination of which 1963 basic
components could be retained; (2) corroboration of the analytical

Front view of the Ford double overhead camshaft engine. (Ford Motor
Co.)

studies on horsepower objectives; (3) a test of the design of the overhead camshaft components; (4) evaluation of the fuel system; and (5) evaluation of the engine-vehicle integration.

Both dynamometer and vehicle testing of this Phase I engine confirmed that the cylinder block and reciprocating and rotating components carried over from the 1963 engine were more than adequate to withstand the highest demands in speeds and loads which would be made by the 1964 competition. These tests also indicated that a four-valve, pent-roof combustion chamber design would permit a peak of more than 400 horsepower to be achieved at approximately 8,000 rpm. The particular combustion chamber of the first design, however, exhibited a deficiency. Dynamometer tests in Dearborn and vehicle tests at Indianapolis confirmed that an engine with a chamber of this design, when using gasoline, would not permit sufficient cooling around the valves. A redesigned chamber was incorporated in the engines subsequently built. Although the objectives called for carburetors, the engineers anticipated difficulty in obtaining the requisite size. Fortunately, fuel injection had been tested at an early stage and this prevented a serious delay when the nonavailability of the carburetors was confirmed. The tests demonstrated rather conclusively that the basic Hilborn injection system, modified for gasoline, would be the final choice. In an actual track comparison between carburetion and fuel injection at Indianapolis, one of the Phase I engines in the race vehicle was tested with the 58 mm Weber carburetors used in 1963 and with the Hilborn fuel-injection system. Both performed equally well, with the Hilborn being slightly superior in fuel economy; however, this latter fact was attributable to a characteristic of the Weber carburetor installation by which Ford was unwittingly penalized in 1963. The Weber carburetors had been designed to have minimum ram length between the entrance to the air horn and the valve. The length used by the Ford engineers produced pulse reversals which backflowed fuel through the carburetor to the airstream, causing a loss of several gallons in the 1963 race.

Installation of the Phase I engine uncovered problems in routing the exhaust ducting around chassis components. Because outside exhaust manifold on an overhead cam V-8 left the engine at a much lower position, some pipes had to be routed through the rear suspension linkage. This awkward and complicated routing led the engineers to interchange the positions of the intake and exhaust systems. The rear-engine location made this possible.

Phase II engines were built primarily to refine the fuel injection and to study whether more than one spark source could improve combustion. Several cylinder heads were built to permit installation of up to three spark plugs per chamber. Distributor arrangements providing selective firing either singularly or in combination gave a very thorough evaluation of combustion characteristics as a function of ignition sources and timing. Dynamometer data showed conclusively that the small power gain which multiple spark plugs might provide could not possibly justify the extreme complication of the electrical system.

The Phase III engine, for all practical purposes, was the Indianapolis race engine; however, design refinements were incorporated almost to race date. For the Phase III engine, six exhaust systems were initially built to meet the requirements of the car builders. Tests at Kingman, Arizona, showed that the valley location of the exhaust was superior because of less aerodynamic drag and better exhaust tuning.

Initially five periods of track testing were scheduled. The first of these was at Indianapolis, October 28–31, 1963, and was for the evaluation of the Phase I engine in a racing chassis and the preliminary assessment of fuel injection in place of carburetion. The results confirmed the basic soundness of the double overhead cam engine for intensive development and the acceptability of the Hilborn fuel-injection system. The results also confirmed several anticipated deficiencies of the initial design and disclosed certain other shortcomings that only a shakedown could uncover. Among these latter were oil and gas leaks and oil pullover via the breather.

The second and third test sessions were held at the Kingman, Arizona, test track January 20–27, and in February, 1964. The purpose of these periods of track testing was to provide confirmation of changes which were made after the Indianapolis tests, all of which had received preliminary validation in dynamometer tests at Dearborn. This track test period also provided the initial shakedown for the Phase III engine and the first comparisons of the new valley exhaust configurations. The results of the January testing period focused attention on the need for a new attack on the oil pullover problem to assure an adequate solution for the maximum sustained load in the higher operating range of the Phase III engine. A solution was found and its effectiveness was confirmed in the February period of testing at Kingman.

The fourth session was at Indianapolis in March, 1964. This provided the first opportunity to assess the overall performance of the Phase III design at the speedway. It also made possible the testing of several engines in the specific vehicles for which they were intended.

Some of the typical refinements which this testing period produced were those associated with calibration of the fuel-injection system for specific engine-vehicle combinations. Dynamometer testing activities were extensive and occurred in each of the three sepa-

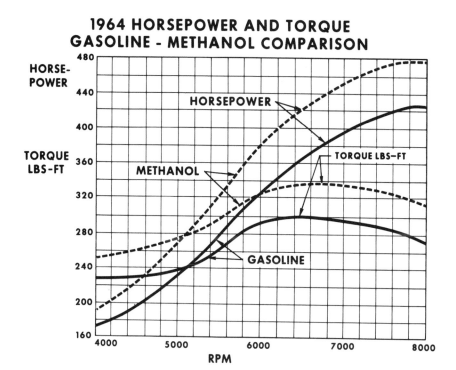

1964 HORSEPOWER AND TORQUE
GASOLINE - METHANOL COMPARISON

rate phases of the program. As a matter of interest, the dynamometer testing in Phase II was sufficiently conclusive to do away with the need for testing the Phase II engine in a vehicle.

The performance phase of the dynamometer development of this engine was concentrated on attaining the objective of 420 horsepower at 8,000 rpm. Once this had been accomplished, concentration was switched to developing the best possible torque curve by varying the cam timing and overlap with several intake manifolds and valve sizes. The desired results were attained with the horsepower peak being 425 at 8,000 rpm and the maximum torque of 295 lbs/ft at 6,400 rpm. At this point of the tests it was decided to determine the increase in performance with methanol as a fuel. The only change made on the engine at this time was to revise the fuel system to handle the increased flow. The results as shown on the chart indicate that close to 475 bhp at 8,000 rpm was achieved with a torque rating of 335 lbs/ft at 6,800 rpm.

It is a fact that with methanol the fuel/air ratio must be rich to overcome its poor octane rating and low heating value. The high heat of vaporization results in internal cooling of the engine. Some engine temperatures recorded at Phoenix showed that when using gasoline with a given installation, 214°F. for the water, 225°F. for the oil were recorded with an ambient temperature of 95°F. Under the same conditions, using methanol, the water temperature was 175°F. and the oil 185°F.

In addition to yielding a great deal of information about the design characteristics, the dynamometer test served in the important evaluation of the durability of the design. In view of the time urgency in the schedule, durability testing had to proceed in parallel with the development testing. A speed and load dynamometer cycle was established on the basis of Indianapolis track data. It consisted of five hours of running at full load with 30-second cycling in the engine speed between 6,300 and 8,100 rpm, in the following sequence and approximate duration:

6,300 to 7,200 rpm in   6 seconds
7,200 to 6,300 rpm in   3 seconds
6,300 to 8,100 rpm in 15 seconds
8,100 to 6,300 rpm in   6 seconds

Six hundred such cycles at full load revealed several sources of possible failure. All were corrected through design changes.

FORD TEST VEHICLE - INDIANAPOLIS TRACK
MARCH 25, 1964 — AVERAGE SPEED 153.8 MPH

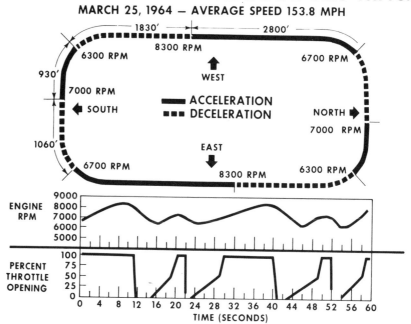

Important technical decisions were based on Indianapolis track acceleration and deceleration characteristics at the outset of the program. A careful analysis was made of the information yielded by the 1963 race entries. Using this as datum in conjunction with the projected increase in engine performance to be achieved with the 1964 engine, it was possible to extrapolate the desired acceleration and deceleration pattern.

The accompanying diagram shows the engine characteristics in one vehicle during the March Indianapolis test, such as the engine speed and throttle opening for a typical circuit of the Indianapolis track. The best average lap speed during this test was 153.8 mph. To accomplish this, the driver reached a peak speed of 183 mph down the straight section of the track, and completed the 2½ miles in slightly more than 58.5 seconds. During this particular lap the engine speed varied between 6,700 and 8,300 rpm on the long straight sections, decreased to 6,300 entering the turns, and reached approximately 7,000 rpm on the short, straight sections between the turns.

ENGINE DEVELOPMENT

A logical point of departure for examining the details of the engine development is provided by a brief description of those elements of the 1963 engine which were retained. It should be remembered that for the Phase I engine, certain features which were initially retained were later discarded, for example, the Weber carburetors. The following references, however, concern only those elements incorporated in the final design.

The engine elements retained from 1963 were: (1) Cylinder block and main bearings; (2) crankshaft (with additional counterweighting); (3) ignition system (mechanical changes in distributor and mounting); (4) alternator; (5) water pump; and (6) oil pan (with new baffling). All these had proved themselves in 1963, and analysis showed that they had the capability of functioning reliably in the higher speed range of the 1964 engine.

In view of the excellent performance of the Ford breakerless ignition system in 1963, it was considered, along with other possible systems. It was adopted for the 1964 engine when it was found to perform satisfactorily at the high speeds required. Certain design refinements were necessary, primarily in the mechanical elements

The 1964 Lotus-Ford, showing the offset suspension. (Indianapolis Motor Speedway)

of the distributor and its external configuration. The operational characteristics of the 1964 engine made it possible to eliminate a spark advance mechanism. The dynamometer determinations of spark requirements established a fixed advance of 52 degrees B.T.C. above 2,000 rpm. A retard device was incorporated for starting purposes. Vehicle testing established a cranking speed of 500 rpm.

Although the engine idles between 2,000 and 2,500 rpm, idling speed could not be fixed at a specific figure, out of deference to the driver. Each driver desires a slightly different feel of the engine response when operating from closed to open throttle in the turns.

Three heat ranges of the Autolite racing spark plugs were found necessary to meet the varying conditions of weather and vehicle calibration.

The new elements of the design were (1) valve gear (including camshafts and associated gear trains and housings); (2) cylinder head with pent-roof combustion chamber (induction and valving);

Installation of the Ford engine in the Lotus chassis. (Indianapolis Motor Speedway)

(3) connecting rods; (4) fuel-injection system; (5) lubrication system (sump pumps and scavenging); and (6) exhaust system.

For the first Phase I engine, operational experience was needed as quickly as possible; consequently, recognized design deficiencies were accepted. For example, there was a definite weakness in this design in that the distributor and fuel-injector drive were mounted at the rear of the camshaft. The torsional windup of the camshaft made a spark scatter beyond anything that was acceptable. The Phase I development testing at Indianapolis made this stand out very clearly. The engine was redesigned to mount these components on the front cover. However, this repositioning required the design of an extremely compact distributor to clear the other vehicle components. This again caused a drive-coupling problem during the durability testing which was finally solved with an intermediate drive shaft splined at each end.

CAMSHAFTS

The camshaft lobe was designed to work against a cup type follower with a cylindrical surface. The camshafts were steel and rode against a steel tappet that had been chrome-plated for wear resistance. There was a bearing for the camshaft in each instance between adjacent cylinders. This tappet required a key, which was visible on the extreme right-hand side of the tappet. It fitted in a groove in the cylinder head and prevented the tappet from rotating. Attempts were made early in the program to run the camshaft without oil holes at each individual cam lobe. This proved to be a mistake, since metal particles were picked up and galling type failures were experienced early in the test cycle. The redesigned camshaft had oil holes drilled in the base circle of each cam, and the camshaft itself was drilled throughout its length.

CAMSHAFT DRIVE

The selection of the method of driving the overhead camshafts was not very difficult. What was required was a very reliable, high-speed drive where cost and noise were not a prime factor; as a result, straight spur gears were the obvious answer. The pushrod engines of 1963 had already established their reliability since they had used steel spur gears for the camshaft, water pump, oil pump, and alternator. It was decided to use this drive system as the basic portion of the gear train and merely add the required gears to complete the camshaft drive. These gears were constructed of steel and were supported by ball bearings in the front cover and gear cover.

The gears, which were bolted to the camshafts, had offset mounting holes to allow for variable cam timing. The gear train included provision for driving the distributor and fuel pump. The camshafts were held in place by aluminum bearing clamps which were secured by two studs. Extensions of these studs provided a mounting for the cam covers. Some consideration was given to alternate gear materials in the interest of weight reduction. However, with reliability a prime factor, the decision was to remain with steel, and defer the study of other materials to future developments.

COMBUSTION CHAMBER

A pent-roof type combustion chamber was used with four valves per cylinder. The spark plug was located in the center portion of the chamber, where maximum burning could occur.

Problems arose over the machining of these combustion chambers to the close tolerances that were required. Ford's Manufacturing Development Group came to the rescue with a technique known as Electrical Discharge Machining (EDM). This technique removes metal by an intermittent high-energy spark from a direct-current source. The spark discharges from an electrode to the workpiece in the presence of a dielectric (oil) solution which covers the workpiece. The metal is removed by the spark through melting and vaporization of a minute volume of the workpiece at the site of the spark impingement.

It was necessary to place cylinder mounting studs on the face of the cylinder head in addition to those on the cylinder block. This was done to prevent the studs from passing through the ports thus

Testing the fuel tank system prior to final assembly. (Indianapolis Motor Speedway)

complicating the head design, while still providing six bolting positions around the combustion chambers. All oil and water passages were sealed with "O" rings which were placed in grooves in the cylinder block. As an added precaution against water leaks, the core support holes on the cylinder face were sealed by welding prior to the machining process.

PISTONS

Great care was taken in the selection of material and design stages to produce maximum strength for minimum weight. For this reason, the piston chosen was an aluminum alloy extrusion. The piston pin was full floating and its length carefully controlled to minimize the impact loading on the pin retainers. The pistons were cam ground, tapered, and fit with 0.007- to 0.008-inch clearance in the bores.

CONNECTING RODS

The connecting rods for the new engine required a new design because of higher loads experienced at higher operating speeds. A comparison of the two designs shows an increase of the piston pin diameter from 0.914 to 0.975 inch. Additional material was added to the bolt boss area of the connecting rod and cap. This was necessary to accommodate the installation of a larger rod bolt, and to provide better rod bearing bore geometry control while operating at the high inertial loads in excess of 8,000 rpm. The overplated copper-lead bearings used in the 1963 engine were retained in the earlier 1964 engine; however, examination of these bearings after being subjected to the higher loads developed at engine speeds in excess of 8,000 rpm gave evidence of possible failure. Accordingly, these bearings were changed to a higher hardness steel backing which could withstand unit stress in the order of 10,000 psi.

FUEL-INJECTION SYSTEM

This aspect of the overall engine design was critical to the attaining of maximum performance. The system was basically a Hilborn, but certain significant design adaptations were incorporated in order to meet the performance criteria established by the development analysis.

Hilborn fuel injection has been widely used but its adoption for the Ford engine was the first instance in which it was employed with gasoline as a fuel in the Indianapolis race. The system provided a continuous fuel flow at relatively low pressure (60 psi maximum line pressure at 8,000 rpm) with good control and wide range of delivery capacity. Accordingly, the delivery requirement of approximately 245 pounds of fuel per hour at 8,000 rpm did not tax the injection system.

Extensive wind tunnel testing was conducted with the fuel-injection system with special attention to its hot-fuel handling capabilities. The tests were conducted at an air speed of 120 mph, and an ambient temperature of 125°F. Air speed, traction force, and road speed were recorded throughout the test, as were the temperatures given by thermocouples installed at various points on the engine. For example, fuel temperatures were recorded going into and coming out of the pump and at the six vehicle tanks. During the most severe run, fuel temperature stabilized at a maximum of 136°F. Since the possibility of vapor lock had to be rigorously assessed, several Reid vapor pressure determinations were made, using five fuel types. No vapor locks were encountered.

The track testing during March yielded the following refinements to the Hilborn installation: (1) Determination of throttle linkage; (2) incorporation of dual economizer valves to improve throttle response during tip-in; and (3) incorporation of a pressure relief and secondary bypass feature to reduce manifold flooding caused by high-speed close-throttle running in the corners.

Other factors bearing upon achieving optimum functioning with the fuel-injection system were fuel specifications, exhaust and induction configuration, and the rubberized fuel cells of the vehicle.

A particular problem that was encountered during the development of the fuel-injection system was noticed during the first weeks of testing at Indianapolis. Flat spots in engine response coming out of the turns were noticed. After considerable investigation, it was determined that the shift in the fuel load through the equalizer line between the left and right tanks under the influence of the accelerating forces in the turns was the cause. Once determined, the correction of the situation was readily accomplished.

LUBRICATION SYSTEM

In the early stages of the development, the system used for the 1963 engine was retained. However, the engineers were aware that the demands imposed on the overhead cam engine would in all probability need revision. The system consisted of a pressure pump to supply oil to the engine, and a scavenge pump which removed oil from the pan and gases from the crankcase and transported these to a sump tank located forward in the vehicle near the oil cooler. When it was found necessary to lubricate each lobe of the camshafts, the pressure pump capacity was increased. This, of course, put a greater demand on the scavenge system, not only in the quantity of oil to be handled, but also in the greater tendency of the oil to foam when draining back from the overhead camshafts through the moving parts of the engine.

In order to cope with the larger demand of oil and air pickup made on the sump pump system, the pump size was increased 100 percent. The pickup tube size was also increased by 50 percent. This was adequate to scavenge the crankcase completely. At Indianapolis trouble was experienced when 8,000 rpm was approached and oil was thrown out of the breather. This problem also occurred at Kingman and was the number one trouble. This oil throwing condition had two principal aspects: first, the oil was subjected to considerable windage by the action of the crankshaft; second, since it was necessary to circulate a large amount of oil through the engine due to large bearing clearances required for lubrication and cooling, this resulted in more throwoff. In addition, the breathing system had to cope with the scavenge pump pulling the air from the crankcase and various cavities within the engine into the sump tank. There was no road draft tube, or outlet air system, as such in the crankcase. The solution was the increasing of the pump and intake tube size, and baffling. A second sump pump was added as further assurance against either failure of the scavenge pump or its inability to handle the increased volume of gas resulting from increased blow-by in the engine.

Jim Clark, Lotus-Ford, Indianapolis, 1964. (Indianapolis Motor Speedway)

The elements of the revised lubrication system included: (1) Redesigned oil pan baffle to control the windage created by the crankshaft and rotating parts; (2) installation of surge baffles to prevent excessive oil in the area of timing gears; (3) better control of the oil to the overhead camshafts; this was accomplished by restricting the quantity of oil to the camshaft lobes and bearings, and installing a return system to prevent oil draining from cylinder heads from being whipped by the rotating parts; (4) increased capacity oil scavenge pump; (5) installation of a second scavenge pump to ensure a more complete pickup of oil from the pan and scavenging of the blow-by gases from the crankcase; and (6) vented sump tank.

A low restriction oil filter was added to the front cover to remove foreign particles which seemed to be ever present in the tubes and connections in the vehicle sump system.

THE EXHAUST SYSTEM

As is well known, much can be done to improve engine performance by suitable tuning of the exhaust system. An exhaust system based on the theoretical tube length of 71.6 inches was

Dan Gurney, Lotus-Ford, Indianapolis, 1964. (Indianapolis Motor Speedway)

developed on the dynamometer. It was decided to pursue a ½ and a ¼ wavelength study, since each of these offered advantages in accommodating the systems to the vehicle. Accordingly, several systems were designed using both the 36-inch and 18-inch tubes. The inboard exhaust systems tested ranged from single pipes to clusters which connected each header separately, all with optimum phasing employing the 36- and 18-inch tube lengths.

Final selection was made of a ½ wavelength pipe with optimum phasing and two divergent collector pipes. This system made vehicle fuel calibration easier and was preferred by the drivers for its apparent improvement in engine response after closed throttle.

The double overhead camshaft engine was ready for the 1964 race and Ford had enough engines to outfit several teams. The factory-sponsored Lotus-Ford team once again comprised Jim Clark and Dan Gurney. These two were backed up by Bobby Marshman who drove the Lotus that Gurney had crashed during practice in 1963. It was fitted with a double overhead camshaft engine in place of the pushrod type Ford and was entered by Lindsey Hopkins as the Pure Oil Special.

The new Ford engines also equipped the Mickey Thompson team of three cars. Two cars with Dave MacDonald and Eddie Johnson as drivers were sponsored by Sears Allstate and the third car with Masten Gregory as driver was sponsored by the Harvey Aluminum Company.

Other Ford-engined cars were the Watson-built Kaiser Aluminum Special of Rodger Ward and the revolutionary Halibrand-Shrike with the cast-magnesium chassis entered as the American Red Ball Special driven by Eddie Sachs.

On May 1, 1964, the Indianapolis track opened for practice and Eddie Sachs made his usual attempt to be first man in action. However, he forgot to turn on the fuel and his Ford engine came to a sudden stop, letting Len Sutton's Offenhauser-engined car beat him for the honor of turning the first lap.

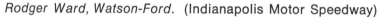

Rodger Ward, Watson-Ford. (Indianapolis Motor Speedway)

Dave MacDonald, Thompson-Ford, Indianapolis, 1964. (Indianapolis
Motor Speedway)

Eddie Johnson, Thompson-Ford, Indianapolis, 1964. (Indianapolis
Motor Speedway)

Eddie Sachs, Halibrand-Ford, Indianapolis, 1964. (Indianapolis Motor
Speedway)

On May 3 Rodger Ward in the Watson-built Ford ran several fast laps, including one at 151.1 mph. Len Sutton was fastest of the Offenhauser brigade at 150.3 mph and the fastest of the conventional roadsters was that of Dick Rathmann at 146.5 mph.

On May 6, A. J. Foyt caused some consternation among the rear-engined devotees when he took his roadster around at 154.189 mph.

Masten Gregory tried one of the Mickey Thompson-Ford streamliners but complained of poor handling because of front-end lift on the straightaway.

On May 7 Parnelli Jones struck another blow for the roadster set when he abandoned his rear-engined car and took his "pet" roadster No. 96 out and turned a sensational lap at 156.22 mph. On May 10 both Rodger Ward and Bobby Marshman were running their Ford-engined cars at satisfactory speeds—Ward at 153.8 mph and Marshman at 153.2 mph.

On May 11 the pace of activity was stepped up with Bobby Unser setting a speed of 154.9 mph in the Novi-Ferguson and the Ford-engined cars finally beginning to show their paces. Marshman turned a lap at 156.1 mph, Rodger Ward followed with 155.4 mph, and Eddie Sachs in the Halibrand-Ford turned 154.6 mph. Jim Clark began his practice but was pulled in when the red light went on due to another car crashing.

On May 12 Marshman was out again with the Lotus-Ford, chief mechanic Jack Beckley having retuned the engine to run on fuel instead of gasoline. After a few laps in the high 155-mph bracket, Marshman turned three laps at over 157 mph, with the fastest one at 157.178 mph. Both Foyt and Jones tried to improve on this with their roadsters but the best roadster time was Foyt's 156.1 mph. On May 14, with qualifications only two days off, everyone was out trying their cars. Rodger Ward clocked 155.8 mph; Jim Clark, 155.4 mph; and Dan Gurney, 154.7 mph.

May 16 was the first day of qualification and Bobby Marshman set the pace of the day with an unofficial practice lap at over 160 mph in the early morning. Eddie Sachs, also doing some last-minute practice, bounded off the wall in the southeast turn and ended his chances of qualifying the Halibrand-Ford on the first day. Jim Clark left no doubt about the potential of the Lotus-Ford when he took pole position with ease, averaging 158.828 mph. Marshman was second fastest at 157.867, and Rodger Ward made it an all-Ford front row with 156.406 mph. Parnelli Jones and A. J. Foyt with the fastest of the roadsters were the next two qualifiers and Dan Gurney filled out the second row with a speed of 154.487 mph. Only one of the Mickey Thompson cars qualified on the first day, Dave MacDonald turning 151.464 for a place in the middle of the fifth row.

On May 17 MacDonald blew his engine, and Eddie Sachs in his repaired car qualified at 151.439 despite a locking brake. There was much speculation about the Lotus-Ford Dunlop tires, as with track temperatures running 132°–137°F. it was seen that Gurney's tires were shredding bits of rubber through the corners. For these tire tests which were held on May 18, Gurney's engine was switched to gasoline and he ran between 151 and 154 mph to simulate expected race speeds.

Gus Scussel of Ford allowed that the use of gasoline would cost about 50 horsepower and would mean that the cars would run up to 4 mph slower. Four of the six Ford engines which qualified were sent back to Dearborn for examination.

On May 19 Eddie Johnson ran the third of the Mickey Thompson-Fords into the wall, which meant that all three Thompson

The pace lap, Ford-engined cars fill the front row. (Indianapolis Motor Speedway)

entries were temporarily out of commission, Gregory's car having been wrecked on May 6 and MacDonald's having a blown engine. After Johnson's car was repaired, he finally qualified at 152.905 mph.

Following the usual preliminaries on race day, Tony Hulman gave the traditional command, "Gentlemen, start your engines," and the field set off on the parade lap.

Clark, Marshman, and Ward drive for the first corner. (John W. Posey)

The pack gathered speed and the Mustang pace car pulled off onto the pit approach. Starter Pat Vidan gave the green flag and Clark, Marshman, and Ward took the dive into the first turn flat out. Clark opened a big lead over the rest, having used the multi-speed gearbox of the Lotus to good effect; Marshman was second and Ward third. A. J. Foyt and Parnelli Jones in their roadsters held fourth and fifth places, while Gurney's Lotus-Ford ran sixth.

Clark leads. (Indianapolis Motor Speedway)

The race is stopped as MacDonald and Sachs collide in flames. (Indianapolis Motor Speedway)

Clark completed his second lap at the record speed of 154 mph and Dan Gurney slipped inside the roadsters to take fourth place.

Then there was chaos. Dave MacDonald's Mickey Thompson entry slid sideways to the inside of the track and exploded into flames against the inner wall; the car bounced back onto the track to be hit broadside by Eddie Sachs. As fire and smoke spread over the track the red flag was out and the race come to a halt.

Clark leads again at the restart. (Robert P. Tronolone)

Gurney and Ward about to lap Bob Wente's roadster. (Indianapolis Motor Speedway)

A chastened crowd watched the resumption of the race an hour and forty-five minutes later. Both MacDonald and Sachs had lost their lives, several others were injured, and 26 of the original 33 cars took the restart.

Clark led off again at a blistering pace and by the end of lap 5 he was already among the tailenders. The heavy traffic slowed Clark and allowed Marshman to close up. The Pure Oil Lotus-Ford went into the lead on lap 7, and on lap 8 Marshman was leading by three seconds from Clark, Gurney, and Ward, with the two roadsters of Foyt and Jones having a tremendous dice behind them. Marshman increased his lead and the average climbed to 153 mph by lap 10.

Gurney pits with fuel-feed problems. (Indianapolis Motor Speedway)

Gurney was the first of the Lotus-Ford to have problems. He came into the pits on lap 19 to have a faulty fuel tank selector attended to. This dropped him to fifteenth place.

Marshman was averaging 154.601 mph and by lap 25 had a 14-second lead. Gurney worked his way back into eighth place by lap 30, at which point Marshman was 23 seconds ahead of Clark.

It was noticed that Marshman was going low on the turns and this caused his downfall. The water and oil pipes scraped on the dirt and as lap 40 neared, oil smoke began to appear from the back of the Lotus-Ford.

Bobby Marshman leads at the record-breaking speed of 154.6 mph. (Robert P. Tronolone)

Clark and Marshman in close company. (Indianapolis Motor Speedway)

Marshman's race ends with broken oil pipes. (John W. Posey)

Clark out on lap 48 with fractured rear suspension. (John W. Posey)

Roger Ward saves the day with a 2d place in his Watson-Ford. (Robert P. Tronolone)

Clark retook the lead on lap 40 as Marshman pulled into the infield on the northwest turn. But his lead was short lived. On lap 48 part of the tread parted from his left tire and the thrashing rubber broke the suspension. Clark showed complete control as he steered his crippled car into the infield. This left the two roadsters of Jones and Foyt to duel for the lead. Ward's Watson-Ford suffered from the same problem which had pitted Gurney the first time, selector valve failure. He was forced to run on partially filled tanks and made many pit stops as the race droned on.

When Jones's car caught fire during refueling, Foyt took over the lead with Ward securely in second place. Colin Chapman called Gurney in on lap 112 to retire the car as he was afraid the same tire failure experienced by Clark would also affect the second Lotus-Ford.

The roadsters won again when Foyt came in first, and Ward's Ford-engined car finished second. But the situation was clear: The rear-engined cars would not have to wait much longer before they dominated the 500-mile race.

CHAPTER 6

Victory at Indianapolis

In 1965 the Lotus-Ford team was back at Indianapolis. Jim Clark again drove the number one team car with rookie Bobby Johns assigned to the number two driving position. Dan Gurney was in the third car of the Lotus-Ford team, which for the race was sponsored by Yamaha and ran as the Yamaha Special.

In all there were seventeen Ford-engined cars in the lineup of qualifiers for the start. Other Lotus-Fords backing up the factory team were those of Parnelli Jones, A. J. Foyt, and Al Miller. Lola-Fords were entered for Bud Tinglestad and Al Unser; BRP-Ford for Masten Gregory and Johnny Boyd; Halibrand-Fords for Lloyd Ruby, Roger McCluskey, Johnny Rutherford, and Joe Leonard. Don Branson drove the single Watson-Ford after Rodger Ward's practice misfortunes with the other, and Len Sutton drove the Vollstedt-Ford.

On May 1 the proceedings began at Indianapolis. Len Sutton

Jim Clark's Lotus-Ford won the 1965 Indianapolis race at record speed. (Indianapolis Motor Speedway)

Masten Gregory, BRP-Ford, Indianapolis, 1965. (Indianapolis Motor Speedway)

Don Branson, Watson-Ford, Indianapolis, 1965. (Indianapolis Motor Speedway)

Joe Leonard, Halibrand-Ford, Indianapolis, 1965. (Indianapolis Motor Speedway)

with the Vollstedt-Ford was first man on the track, but nothing spectacular in the way of speed was recorded as there was a 150-mph limit imposed for the first three days. On May 4 the limit was lifted and the drivers began to get in the groove. Foyt, Sutton, and Ruby in Ford-engined cars all ran at over 154 mph.

On May 5 A. J. Foyt crashed his Lotus-Ford when the rear hub carrier broke on the backstretch. The car spun, tore off the left wheel, and damaged the nose.

The 1965 pole (r. to l.) A. J. Foyt; a mechanic subs for Clark; Dan Gurney. (Indianapolis Motor Speedway)

Len Sutton, Vollstedt-Ford, Indianapolis, 1965. (Indianapolis Motor Speedway)

Rodger Ward's Watson-Ford.
(Indianapolis Motor Speedway)

Rear view of the Watson-Ford.
(Indianapolis Motor Speedway)

The following day the USAC Technical Committee temporarily grounded six cars that used hub carriers similar to those on Foyt's car, insisting that these carriers be strengthened. Before this went into effect, Clark turned several laps at over 154 mph in his Lotus-Ford.

By May 7 the problems were sorted out and Clark turned the fastest lap of the day at 156.5 mph. The Scot following up the next day with 158.92 mph. Rodger Ward, the two-times Indianapolis winner, experienced trouble with his Watson-Ford all week and had further bad luck when a bearing seized and his engine blew.

Monday, May 10, saw the arrival of several more Ford-engined cars, including those of Gurney and Hurtubise. Foyt recorded the fastest lap of the day at 158.3 mph.

On Tuesday, May 11, Foyt upped his speed to 159.943 mph and finally broke through the 160-mph barrier on Thursday with a speed of 161.146 mph, Clark being close behind with 160.142.

First day of qualification was on Saturday, May 15. Len Sutton with the Vollstedt-Ford was the first to qualify with a four-lap

Old favorite Jim Hurtubise on qualification day. (Indianapolis Motor Speedway)

Hurtubise's car after his qualification attempt. (Indianapolis Motor Speedway)

Mario Andretti, Brawner-Ford, Indianapolis, 1965. (Indianapolis Motor Speedway)

Mario Andretti removes his rookie stripes while car builder Clint Brawner watches. (Indianapolis Motor Speedway)

average of 156.121 mph. Nine cars followed Sutton before rookie Mario Andretti brought the Dean Van Lines Brawner-Ford to the line for his qualification attempt. As he turned the first lap at 159.179 mph the crowd rose to its feet; his four-lap average of 158.849 was a new 10-mile record. While Andretti was being congratulated, Jim Clark's green-and-yellow Lotus-Ford was on the track and proceeded to demolish Andretti's record, setting a new one with an average of 160.729 mph.

Clark's run was immediately followed by A. J. Foyt, and again the record was broken with an average of 161.233 mph, a speed which was good enough to guarantee pole position.

Lloyd Ruby's Halibrand-Ford qualified at 157.246 mph. (Indianapolis Motor Speedway)

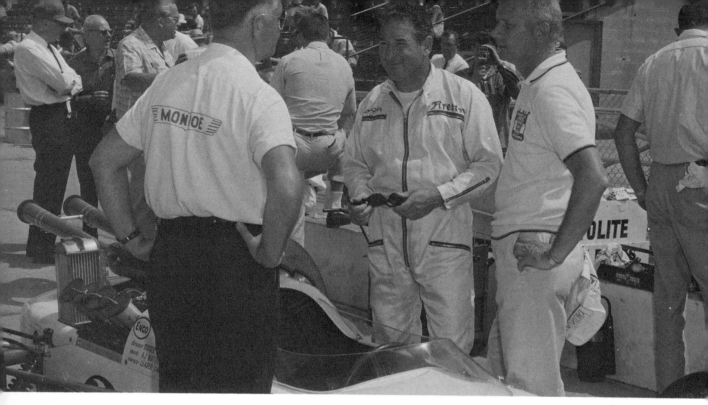

Two-time winner Rodger Ward had many misadventures and did not qualify for the 1965 race. (Indianapolis Motor Speedway)

Dan Gurney was the next to qualify, and his average of 158.898 with the Yamaha-entered car made certain of an all-Lotus-Ford front row for the start and relegated Andretti to the second row.

Parnelli Jones's 158.624 mph with the Agajanian-Hurst Lotus-Ford put him next to Andretti. Al Miller and Lloyd Ruby qualified for places in the third row.

On Saturday, May 12, only one car was needed to complete the field, and Rodger Ward made another effort with his recalcitrant Watson-Ford. The attempt proved abortive when Ward crashed on the backstretch on his warming-up lap and he had to sit out his first 500-mile race in fifteen years.

One of Ward's problems—a blown engine (John W. Posey)

Another of Ward's problems—too close contact with the wall. (Indianapolis Motor Speedway)

130

The pace lap. Foyt, Clark, An-dretti, Parnelli Jones. (Socony
Mobil Oil Co., Inc.)

Masten Gregory's BRP-Ford passes two Offy-engined cars. (Indianapolis Motor Speedway)

A look at the field of 33 showed 27 rear-engined cars, of which 17 were Ford-powered and 10 Offenhauser-powered, plus 4 Offenhauser roadsters and 2 front-engined Novis.

On Memorial Day, 1965, the 49th running of the Indianapolis 500 was under way. As the pace car pulled off and the green flag fell, Jim Clark jumped into the lead with A. J. Foyt and Dan Gurney close behind. On lap 2 Foyt forged ahead of Clark, who promptly retook the lead on lap 3.

The first lap. Foyt leads Clark,
Gurney, and Parnelli Jones.
(Socony Mobil Oil Co., Inc.)

Heavy traffic—Foyt has passed three tail-enders. Gurney (17) and Jones (98) look for a way through. (Indianapolis Motor Speedway)

Clark (82) and Andretti (12) working through traffic. (Indianapolis Motor Speedway)

Johnny Boyd, BRP-Ford, leads Bud Tinglestad, Lola-Ford. (Robert P. Tronolone)

The speed announced for lap 1 was 151.380 mph, a new record. At the end of 10 laps the order was Clark, Foyt, Gurney, Parnelli Jones, Al Miller, and Mario Andretti, six Ford-engined cars holding the first six positions.

The first Ford in trouble was that of Lloyd Ruby, who spun on the northwest turn and ran into the infield. He made for the pits to check the car over and then rejoined the race.

Bud Tinglestad loses a wheel from his Lola-Ford. (Indianapolis Motor Speedway)

Parnelli Jones makes a pit stop while in third place. (Indianapolis Motor Speedway)

At lap 20 the order remained the same except that Andretti had moved up to fifth ahead of Miller.

At lap 50 Clark still led Foyt by over 10 seconds, with Parnelli Jones third and Andretti now up to fourth. Clark's speed at lap 50 was 152.153 mph, over 5 mph faster than the previous year's record. Then came the pit stops. Parnelli Jones was in for fuel on lap 63, taking 45 seconds. Clark pitted on lap 66 and was out again in the phenomenal time of 19.8 seconds.

Lloyd Ruby brings his Halibrand-Ford in for refueling. (Indianapolis Motor Speedway)

Al Unser makes his pit stop with the Lola-Ford. (Indianapolis Motor Speedway)

Foyt passed into the lead during Clark's pit stop but on lap 75 he too had to stop for fuel. His stop time of 44.3 seconds wiped out any advantage he might have had over Clark and the new Lotus-Ford was back in the lead.

At the end of lap 100 the order was Clark, Foyt, Jones, and Andretti, with Clark setting a new record of 152.18 mph compared to the old record of 146.962 set by Foyt in 1964. On lap 114 Foyt pulled into the pits, his race over with a blown engine.

By lap 130 Clark was securely in first place with a 2-minute lead over Parnelli Jones. He pitted for the second time on lap 136 and refueled in 24.7 seconds. After his pit stop he still had a lead of 1 min. 31 sec. over Jones and at lap 150 Clark again set a new record of 151.138 mph compared to the previous year's speed of 146.897 mph.

Masten Gregory moved up to 5th before retiring. (Robert P. Tronolone)

Parnelli Jones took 2d place in the Agajanian-Hurst-Lotus-Ford. (Ford Motor Co.)

A. J. Foyt, retired with a blown engine, was classified 15th. (Indianapolis Motor Speedway)

Mario Andretti was named "Rookie of the Year" with 3d place. (Ford Motor Co.)

Len Sutton with the Vollstedt-Ford finished 12th. (Robert P. Tronolone)

Al Miller's Lotus-Ford took 4th place. (Indianapolis Motor Speedway)

Bobby Johns drove the backup Lotus-Ford into 7th Place. (Robert P. Tronolone)

Jim Clark with his crew. (John W. Posey)

Clark crossed the finishing line followed by Parnelli Jones and rookie of the year, Mario Andretti. The first three cars all broke the previous record, Clark's new figure being 150.686 mph. In fourth place was the Lotus-Ford of Al Miller, making it a clean sweep for the Ford-engined cars.

Activities for the 1966 Indianapolis 500 began on April 30
with Mario Andretti driving the Mercury pace car through the
official speedway banner. Roger McCluskey in the Lindsey Hopkins
Lotus-Ford was the first on the track and he completed the first lap
of the season under the yellow caution light.

On May 1 Jackie Stewart began his rookie test in the John
Mecom Lola-Ford while a 150-mph limit was set by Chief Steward
Harlan Fengler. As a result of this there were no exceptional times
during the day.

*The front row for 1966 (r. to l.) Mario Andretti, a mechanic subs for
Clark, George Snider.* (Indianapolis Motor Speedway)

*Victory at Indianapolis. Jim
Clark and the Lotus-Ford.* (Indianapolis Motor Speedway)

On May 2 the 150-mph limit was still in force and Joe Leonard and Carl Williams were reprimanded by the chief steward when they both turned laps at over that speed.

On May 3 it was announced that 1962 World Driving Champion Graham Hill would replace the late Walt Hansgen at the wheel of the American Red Ball Special Lola-Ford owned by John Mecom Jr. With the 150-mph limit lifted, several drivers attempted speed runs, the fastest of the day being Joe Leonard in the Yamaha Eagle-Ford at 157.563 mph.

On May 4 Jackie Stewart passed his rookie test and was given approval to compete by the Indianapolis Drivers Committee. Jim Clark made his first runs with the STP Oil Treatment Lotus-Ford.

On May 5 Mario Andretti became the first driver to break the 160-mph mark in 1966, with a lap at 160.657 mph.

European Grand Prix driver Jackie Stewart removes his rookie stripes after passing his tests. (Indianapolis Motor Speedway)

Graham Hill, Lola-Ford, Indianapolis, 1966. (Indianapolis Motor Speedway)

The following day other drivers made some fast runs. A. J. Foyt in the Coyote-Ford ran 157.978 mph; Jim Clark, 157.0 mph; and Carl Williams in the Gerhardt-Ford, 157.8 mph.

On Sunday, May 8, Andretti gave an indication of the pace that could be expected in qualification when he turned 163.3 mph in his Brawner-Ford, and Carl Williams made 160.4 mph in his Gerhardt-Ford. The following day Clark posted a time of 162.984 mph, but Andretti was in great form and recorded 164.926 mph.

On May 11 a wet track kept anyone from running until noontime, but later in the day Andretti caused a sensation with a lap at 167.5 mph. He was followed by Clark at 165.7 mph and Gurney at 164.8 mph.

Qualification day, Friday May 13, was highlighted by Andretti's 168.5 mph warm-up lap and 165.899 mph four-lap average to take the pole position.

On the pole—Mario Andretti, car owner Al Dean, chief mechanic Clint Brawner, and team. (Indianapolis Motor Speedway)

Billy Foster, Vollstedt-Ford, Indianapolis, 1966. Indianapolis Motor Speedway)

Jerry Grant, Eagle-Ford, Indianapolis, 1966. (Indianapolis Motor Speedway)

Jim Clark turned down speeds of 164 mph plus during the day hoping to displace Andretti, but finally settled for a four-lap average of 164.144 mph in the late afternoon to sit beside Andretti in the first row. Third man in the front row was George Snider, who averaged 162.521 in his Lotus-Ford.

Lloyd Ruby qualified the Eagle-Ford for the second row and Gordon Johncock placed his Gerhardt-Ford next to Ruby.

The third row was made up of Jim McElreath, Moore-Ford; Chuck Hulse, Watson-Ford; and Don Branson, Gerhardt-Ford. Row four had Jackie Stewart, Lola-Ford, alongside Jerry Grant's Eagle-Ford, and the fifth row had Johnny Boyd, BRP-Ford, and Graham Hill, Lola-Ford. At the end of the first day of qualification the Ford-engined cars dominated the field without question.

One of the several casualties of the first qualification day was A. J. Foyt, who ran his Coyote-Ford into the wall just before he was due to make his qualification run.

On the second day of qualification A. J. Foyt switched to his Lotus-Ford and set the fastest time of the day at 161.355 mph and the Eagle-Fords of Dan Gurney and Joe Leonard qualified at 160.499 and 159.560 mph, respectively.

A. J. Foyt wrecked his No. 2 Coyote-Ford just before qualification. (Indianapolis Motor Speedway)

Chuck Hulse, Watson-Ford, Indianapolis, 1966. (Indianapolis Motor Speedway)

Graham Hill waits patiently before the start. (Indianapolis Motor Speedway)

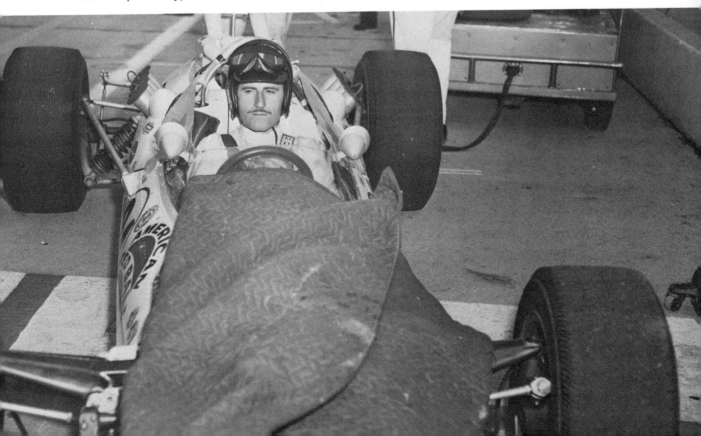

Lloyd Ruby, Eagle-Ford, Indianapolis, 1966. (Indianapolis Motor Speedway)

Foyt switched to his reserve car, No. 45 Lotus-Ford for qualification. (Indianapolis Motor Speedway)

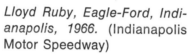

George Snider qualified for the front row with a Lotus-Ford at 162.521 mph. (Indianapolis Motor Speedway)

Jim Clark's Lotus-Ford sponsored by STP for 1966. (STP Corporation)

Jim Clark looks pleased with his 164.144 mph for a front-row position. (Indianapolis Motor Speedway)

Jackie Stewart, Lola-Ford, Indianapolis, 1966, with chief mechanic George Bignotti. (Indianapolis Motor Speedway)

Dan Gurney consults with chief steward Harlan Fengler before quali-fication. (Indianapolis Motor Speedway)

Dan Gurney qualified his Eagle-Ford at 160.499 mph. (John W. Posey)

The flag falls and the front row heads for the first corner. (In-dianapolis Motor Speedway)

The pace lap. (Indianapolis Motor Speedway)

Saturday, May 21 was the last day of qualifying and five more Ford-engined cars made the field for a total of 24 cars out of 33.

At 10:55 A.M. on race day Indianapolis Speedway owner Tony Hulman said, as he had for the previous twenty years, "Gentlemen, start your engines." All but one car crept forward and followed the pace car.

As the green flag was dropped, the front-row starters made their frantic dive for the first turn, but attention was attracted

As Snider has slight lead chaos begins in the middle of the field.
(Indianapolis Motor Speedway)

Cars and wheels fly in every direction. (Indianapolis Motor Speedway)

immediately to the middle of the field where flying wheels and metal parts were the indication of a monumental pile-up. Sixteen drivers were involved in a mass crash that apparently began when Billy Foster's Vollstedt-Offy touched Gordon Johncock's Gerhardt-Ford. The mishap took place at 11:02 A.M., but by 11:12 Dr. Thomas Hannah, chief of the speedway medical staff, announced that no one was hurt aside from scratches and small cuts.

Eliminated by the accident were Don Branson, Gerhardt-Ford; A. J. Foyt, Lotus-Ford; Dan Gurney, Eagle-Ford; Arnie Knepper, Cecil-Ford; Al Miller, Lotus-Ford; Cale Yarborough, Vollstedt-Ford; Larry Dickson, Halibrand-Ford; Ronnie Duman, Eisert-Ford, together with three Offy-engined cars.

The race was delayed 1 hour and 24 minutes so that all the wreckage could be removed and the track cleaned. The cars restarted in single file, according to the order in which they were at the time of the accident.

At the end of lap 1 it was Andretti, Clark, and Snider in Ford-engined cars followed by Parnelli Jones in the supercharged Halibrand-Offy. The Ford-powered cars of Ruby, McElreath, Hulse, Grant, and Stewart, running fifth, sixth, seventh, eighth, and ninth, respectively. Almost immediately the yellow caution light was on as Johnny Boyd hit the wall in the south straight with his BRP-Ford and lost two wheels.

The remains of Foyt's car after the lap-1 pile-up. (Indianapolis Motor Speedway)

The remains of Gurney's Eagle-Ford after the lap-1 pile-up. (Indianapolis Motor Speedway)

Only a few minutes after the restart Johnny Boyd crashed his BRP-Ford into the wall. (Indianapolis Motor Speedway)

At lap 10 Andretti still led from Clark and Snider, but the average was only 116.991 mph due to the yellow light.

On lap 17 Clark took the lead and on lap 24 Andretti was in the pits for a new set of goggles. The average speed crept up to 130.795 mph but the yellow light was on again when second-place George Snider collided with Chuck Hulse.

Andretti pitted again on lap 25 to change spark plugs, losing 1 minute 44 seconds, and Jackie Stewart was in the pits for a new set of goggles.

On lap 30 Andretti was in again. His pit reported valve trouble and the car was pushed to the garage area.

At lap 50 it was Clark, Ruby, Jones with the Halibrand-Offy; McElreath, Ward with a Lola-Offy; followed by the Ford-engined cars of McCluskey, Grant, Stewart, and Hill.

At lap 60 there were only two Offy-engined cars in the first 10, running in third and ninth places. The average speed increased to 140.879 mph.

On lap 65 Jim Clark spun in the fourth corner and headed for the pits to have his tires checked. Lloyd Ruby took the Eagle-Ford into the lead.

Clark made use of his pit stop to take on fuel and change two tires. He was in for 20.5 seconds and regained the lead when Ruby refueled on lap 76.

At lap 80 Ford-engined cars held the first six places, Parnelli Jones having dropped back to seventh, finally retiring with a damaged wheel bearing.

Clark spun again and once more pitted to check the tires, rejoining the race in third place behind Ruby and Stewart. Clark moved back into second as Stewart pitted on lap 131 and regained the lead on the same lap as Ruby also made a pit stop for a tire change and to take on fuel.

On lap 139 Clark was running at a slower pace and Ruby retook the lead at the end of the main straight.

On lap 145 Clark pitted again for 22 seconds to take on fuel. Ruby's car began to smoke heavily and he was black-flagged at the end of lap 152, which gave the lead to Stewart.

At lap 180 it was Jackie Stewart, Lola-Ford; Graham Hill, Lola-Ford; Jim Clark, Lotus-Ford; Jim McElreath, Moore-Ford; and Gordon Johncock, Gerhardt-Ford in the first five positions. As the yellow light had been on for a total of 41 minutes, the average speed was only 144.261 mph.

On lap 192 Stewart was seen to be dropping below the white line with the engine off in the third turn, and as the Scot headed toward the pits with a blown engine, Graham Hill took over the lead with eight laps to go.

As the last of the 200 laps came to an end, it was Graham Hill the victor, followed by Jim Clark, Jim McElreath, Gordon Johncock,

George Snider's Lotus-Ford finished 19th. (John W. Posey)

Jim McElreath's Brabham-Ford finished 3d. (Indianapolis Motor Speedway)

Jim Clark finished 2d after two spins. (Indianapolis Motor Speedway)

Graham Hill waves to the crowd. (Indianapolis Motor Speedway)

and Mel Kenyon in the first of the Offy-powered cars and the unlucky Stewart classified sixth.

There was a mixup at the finish as both Graham Hill and Jim Clark headed for victory lane. Clark's pits had been informing him that he held first place. When Hill was declared the winner Granatelli of STP protested, but the records proved that Clark's pit crew had made a very expensive mistake. Hill's average speed was 144.317 mph, some 6 mph slower than Clark's average in 1965.

Graham Hill, winner of the 1966 Indianapolis 500-mile race. (Indianapolis Motor Speedway)

The Indianapolis 500 Mile Race of 1967 again proved to be a Ford sweep. Ford-engined cars took the first five places, but it was not as easy a victory as it seems from the record. The new STP Turbine car dominated the race, and had it not been for a last minute bearing failure in the Turbine's transmission the Ford-engined cars would have been decisively defeated.

The month of May started well enough for the Ford-engined cars. There seemed to be little challenge from the turbocharged and positive displacement supercharged Offenhausers, but old hands at Indianapolis noticed the smooth performance of the Turbine—its great acceleration, maximum speed and cornering ability. The Turbine's total lap speeds, however, were not up to those of the Fords, and transmission bearing troubles in practice caused most people to discount it as an actual threat.

Denis Hulme, the 1967 World Champion, Eagle-Ford, Indianapolis, 1967. (Indianapolis Motor Speedway)

Gordon Johncock in No. 3 Gerhardt-Ford practices refueling. (Indianapolis Motor Speedway)

The All-American Racers crew practice wheel changing on Dan Gurney's Eagle-Ford. (Indianapolis Motor Speedway)

Qualification speeds comfortably exceeded those of 1966 and Mario Andretti once again took pole position with his Brawner-Ford at an average speed of 168.928 mph. On the front row with him were Dan Gurney in his Eagle-Ford at 167.224 mph and Gordon Johncock with a Gerhardt-Ford at 166.559 mph. The second row included two more Ford-engined cars, A. J. Foyt with the Coyote-Ford at 166.289 mph and Joe Leonard with another Coyote-Ford at 166.098 mph. Parnelli Jones driving the STP Turbine car went faster than he had in practice and took the third place in the second row at 166.075 mph. The third row was occupied by the first of the Offy-engined cars, Lloyd Ruby qualifying at 165.229 mph; but he was flanked by two more Ford-engined cars, those of the Unser brothers, Bobby and Al. Two more Fords, George Snider's and Jim McElreath's, were in the third row.

Jerry Grant and Dan Gurney (in car) discuss the performance of the stock block Ford-Gurney-Weslake engine used in Eagle No. 48. (Indianapolis Motor Speedway)

The 1967 front row pose with Andretti's pole-winning car. (l. to r.) Andretti, 168.982 mph; Gurney, 167.224 mph; Johncock, 166.559 mph, all with Ford-engined cars. (Indianapolis Motor Speedway)

The best that 1966-winner Graham Hill could do with his STP Lotus-Ford was to qualify for the eleventh row at 163.317 mph and Jim Clark, the 1965 winner, also with an STP Lotus-Ford qualified for the sixth row at 163.213 mph; neither of these cars were really well prepared as the efforts of the STP team were behind the Turbine car.

Al Unser, Lola-Ford, Indianapolis, 1967. (Indianapolis Motor Speedway)

An unhappy Jim Clark ponders on his 163.213 mph qualifying speed, slower than his time in 1966. (Indianapolis Motor Speedway)

The pace lap, 1967. (Indianapolis Motor Speedway)

The rush for the first turn. Andretti leads Johncock and Gurney. The STP turbine (left) positions itself to pass all three on the first lap. (Indianapolis Motor Speedway)

Rain threatened as the cars circulated behind the pace car, preparing for the start of the race. As the green flag fell Mario Andretti in the Brawner-Ford took the lead from pole position. Only seconds later Parnelli Jones in the STP Turbine pushed his way into the lead from the second row and showed how much the car had been underestimated by some people.

Rain started to spatter the race track as Parnelli Jones increased his lead, and after about 45 miles of running, the rain fell in earnest. After consultation, officials decided to stop the race, and for the first time in two generations, the Indy race was held over another day before completion. Fans, mechanics, and officials produced all kinds of improvised shelter. All over the speedway, random corners

of clear plastic flapped in the strong wind that came with the rain. USAC officials delayed announcing the postponement until late in the day, but after two hours of waiting, it was clear that the race would have to be put off.

For some the delay was a windfall. Mario Andretti, who had experienced clutch trouble almost from the start of the race, had a day's grace in which his mechanics worked to repair the Brawner-Ford. A ruling for 1967 had allowed pit crews to work on the cars during unforeseen delays in the race.

The second day saw the restart with the cars lining up in the order they had held on lap 18. As a result of the restart, Parnelli Jones's Turbine car lost most of its lead over second-place-holder Foyt's Coyote Ford.

After two laps the pace car pulled off onto the pit apron, and Jones immediately ran away from the field to establish a lead of almost half a lap with 20 seconds in hand. This set the pattern for most of the race, as the four-wheel-drive Turbine car easily held a commanding lead. The four-wheel drive gave better handling than the Fords, and Jones was able to drive into the corners low, off the "groove" imposed on the other cars.

Lloyd Ruby's turbocharged Offy had retired before the rain halted the race on the previous day, so he took over teammate George Snider's car for the restart. The first car out on the second day was that of Graham Hill, the former World Champion who had won the 1966 event. His Lotus-Ford rolled into the pits with a burned piston on lap 23.

Attrition among the big name drivers continued, with 1965-winner Jim Clark, being next to drop out of the race. On lap 35 his Lotus-Ford came in with an oil leak, after covering only 87.5 miles without ever being in contention for the lead.

The rains came and forced postponement of the 1967 race after 18 laps. (Indianapolis Motor Speedway)

Mario Andretti, pressing hard to make up time after starting at the back of the field, lost a wheel and suddenly spun into the infield, barely missing the second corner wall. Later Andretti attributed his retirement to hard braking, saying that the aluminum-magnesium alloy wheel had expanded from brake heat and slipped off the hub.

Jones had to turn aside to miss a near accident on lap 70 and saved his position by holding his spin to just one turn. Such was the Turbine's lead that he drove into the next corner at an off-line approach and still maintained his first place in an impressive manner.

Another Indy veteran, Al Miller, was black flagged during lap 73 as he was dropping oil. This brought the total number of disabled cars to five.

On lap 79 Parnelli Jones came into the pits for the first of the two mandatory pit stops and Foyt, who had held second place, took the lead.

There was confusion in the pits because Jones was waved away before the fueling hoses were completely disconnected from the car. The pit stop took 36 seconds, and Jones was back in the race, leaving behind torn fuel hoses and disrupted kerosene tanks. He had been leading by 26.2 seconds when he pitted. On lap 83 Foyt's pit crew called in the Coyote-Ford for refueling. At the same time, Carl Williams in a BRP-Ford spun into the infield. Bob Veith damaged his nose cone on the northwest wall. Jerry Grant's Eagle-Ford and Art Pollard's Gerhardt-Offy spun without hitting anything.

Foyt and Al Unser came into their pits at about the same time on lap 83. Jones, only a few seconds behind Foyt's Coyote-Ford, again took the lead. The Turbine car had no difficulty in pulling away from the rest of the field. Foyt's pit stop was a quick 26.9 seconds and he reentered the race in third place.

Dan Gurney, Eagle-Ford, comes in to refuel during the race. (Indianapolis Motor Speedway)

Mario Andretti lost a wheel after 58 laps. (Indianapolis Motor Speedway)

Lee Roy Yarbrough in No. 52 Laycock-Ford during practice. (Indianapolis Motor Speedway)

Other drivers began making their stops; Grim, Stewart, and Kenyon all headed for the pits before lap 88, while Bud Tingle-stadt's Gerhardt-Ford started to smoke badly. Leading Foyt for four laps, Art Pollard spun out on the fourth corner but was able to restart with some help. Parnelli Jones, again in the lead, had completed 78 laps. The yellow flag was still out due to the host of spins. Joe Leonard pulled his Coyote-Ford into the pits for a surprise 11.2-second stop. He had taken a piece of paper into the radiator air duct and wanted it removed to avoid any chance of overheating. This stop may well have cost him second place as this was the only difficulty he had with his otherwise well-running car.

Joe Leonard, Coyote-Ford, 3d in the 1967 Indianapolis 500. (Indianapolis Motor Speedway)

Roger McCluskey, Eagle-Ford, Indianapolis, 1967. (Indianapolis Motor Speedway)

After lap 80 the track record was broken. Foyt's speed was 157.217 mph compared to Jim Clark's 1965 record of 151.574 mph for the same distance. At lap 80 the lead group was Foyt, Jones, Pollard, Cale Yarborough, Stewart, and Kenyon and it was Ford, Turbine, Offy, Ford, Ford, and Offy.

As the race went on, Jones pulled back into the lead after Foyt's lap-83 pit stop. Lap times were over 158 mph, even with the yellow flag out. On lap 89 Jochen Rindt's Eagle with the stock-block Gurney-Weslake-Ford engine began to smoke badly. On lap 89 Dallenbach suffered from a jammed accelerator and hit the wall losing a wheel.

One hundred laps had now passed for Parnelli Jones, as well as for the rest of the lead. He had led for all but four laps. At lap 100 it was Jones, Gurney, Foyt, McCluskey, Pollard, Al Unser, Bobby Unser, Gordon Johncock, Jim McElreath, and Joe Leonard.

Turbine, Ford, Ford, Ford, Offy, Ford, Ford, Ford, Ford, and Ford —the situation looked promising. Average speed was 155.021 mph, but at this point, Dan Gurney headed for his pits. Carl Williams, damaged earlier in the race, came out of his pits with the nose cone removed. Shortly after, a screwdriver fell from the open panels and was spotted by one of the track officials; the yellow flag was put out again so that it could be cleared off the track.

Cale Yarborough spun across the track at the north turn and barely missed taking Chuck Hulse with him. Two other cars, those of Lloyd Ruby and Lee Roy Yarbrough, were involved in an accident as they tried to avoid the spinning car of Cale Yarborough. Lee Roy went into the infield, as Cale restarted and headed for the pits for a quick check-over before returning to the race. Ruby and Lee Roy Yarbrough got out of their cars to take a look while the track crew stood by. Yarbrough helped Ruby restart his car but had to abandon his own as it was too badly damaged.

The green flag was out again briefly, and almost immediately Johnny Rutherford crashed into the wall at the second turn. After lap 103 his Eagle-Ford was too badly damaged to continue.

On lap 111 the green flag was out again. Al Unser, in the pits for tires, lost his third place. Jones was again lapping the tail end of the field, passing Art Pollard and Ronnie Duman. Jones turned lap times at over 160 mph. The Turbine continued to pull away from the field and extended its lead to over a lap.

Stewart pressing hard pulled ahead of Foyt and the two fought it out for three laps.

On lap 128 Roger McCluskey ran out of fuel and just managed to make the pits.

On lap 130—325 miles—Parnelli Jones's pit crew signaled him that they were ready for a stop. On lap 131 he pulled in and Foyt

Joe Leonard's extra pit stop with the Coyote-Ford cost him a possible second place. (Indianapolis Motor Speedway)

once again took over the lead. Jones's stop went much better than the first attempt and he was out in 32.1 seconds. Foyt at this point held a lead of 31 seconds, but Jones and the Turbine had made their last pit stop. Stewart moved up into third place with the Lola-Ford and Gurney was back in the pits with engine problems. Joe Leonard, holding down fifth place, also made a stop to take on new tires.

Foyt, in the lead, was turning times faster than some of the earlier ones of the Turbine car. His lap-130 speed was 160.5 mph.

Al Unser and Jackie Stewart fought it out with Foyt for several laps as Foyt's pit crew was preparing for the Coyote-Ford's last pit stop.

Stewart and Foyt pitted within a few seconds of each other, while Jones once again took the lead on lap 150. Foyt's lead of 22.8 seconds was eaten up fast by the Turbine, and Jones established himself with a 19.4 second lead.

Arnie Knepper, Cecil-Ford, Indianapolis, 1967. (Indianapolis Motor Speedway)

A. J. Foyt, Coyote-Ford, winner of the 1967 Indianapolis 500. (Indianapolis Motor Speedway)

Gurney, now far behind in the standings, passed Al Unser and A. J. Foyt on lap 154, but his exhaust was sounding rougher and rougher. Gurney pitted again and stayed for 39.8 seconds, while Foyt returned to the race in 26.7 seconds and continued to hold second place. Dan Gurney was finally black flagged as his engine was smoking too heavily and was losing oil.

Roger McCluskey was also flagged off with engine trouble on lap 165 after completing 405 miles.

Seconds after Jones lapped Jackie Stewart, the Scot's car pulled off into the infield. The engine of the Lola-Ford had blown after completing 420 miles.

Arnie Knepper with the Cecil-Ford brushed the wall, but kept control and continued in the race. Jones, at this point, held a 34-second lead.

With nineteen laps to go, Jones still led as Mel Kenyon and Cale Yarborough spun close together and hit the wall, putting both cars out of the race.

Parnelli Jones's lap-180 speed was 152.982 mph, another new record.

The two crashes had brought out the yellow flag and the green was out again with nine laps to go.

On the third turn, Gordon Johncock lost a wheel and spun. He avoided the wall and brought the car to a stop as the yellow light went on again.

At lap 195 the yellow light was still on. Jones had five laps to go. His speed was 152.982 mph, again breaking the lap record held by Jim Clark at 150.996 mph.

On lap 197 it happened: Jones coasted into the pits as the crowd rose to its feet with a deafening roar. The Turbine had broken a ball bearing in its power transfer transmission. Foyt passed the scene of gloom in the Granatelli-STP pits, taking the lead with only two laps to go. The yellow light was still on around the track as Foyt was given the white flag informing him that he had one lap left to complete.

Suddenly, three cars—ahead of Foyt but behind him in the standings—ran together in a wild melee of flying wheels and flaming fuels. Carl Williams, Chuck Hulse, and Bobby Grim were the drivers involved. Foyt, rounding the home stretch turn to take the checkered flag, came up on the gyrating mess. He shifted into low gear and weaved the Coyote-Ford through the spinning cars. He was given the checkered flag by the back-up starter as the chief starter, Pat Vidan, waved both yellow and red flags to stop the other cars. Miraculously, no one was hurt, and the 1967 Indianapolis 500 Mile Race ended with another Ford victory. It had been touch and go, and it was obvious that the Turbines if permitted in future races could well end the reign of the Ford-engined cars at Indianapolis.

CHAPTER 7

The GT Project

After it was definitely decided that Ford was going to go racing, Henry Ford II and Lee Iacocca came up with the idea to buy out Ferrari. The reasoning behind this was to get into international racing as quickly as possible and the experience, facilities, and brains were available under one roof at Ferrari. This decision was made in January, 1963, and in May, Phil Paradise, head of Ford's Italian organization approached Ferrari.

The proposal was to form two companies: one was to be Ford-Ferrari with Ford as the major stockholder, its purpose being to construct and sell the luxury Gran Turismo (GT) and sports cars that Ferrari was already manufacturing. The other was to be Ferrari-Ford with Ferrari the majority stockholder. This was to be the racing company, with Ferrari basically running the show but Ford making use of the publicity and engineering developments that resulted from the racing activity.

The arrangement seemed to be satisfactory to both Ferrari and Ford and Donald Frey, Ford Division's general manager, took a team of business specialists to Modena to begin the official negotiations in mid-May. Negotiations went well until questions of Shelby-American, Formula 1, and GT racing came up. Ferrari felt that there would be a conflict of interest with Shelby-American and wanted Ford to sever relations with that company.

Ford's lack of interest in Formula 1 at that time was understandable as the Federation Internationale de l'Automobile limit for the world championship category was 1.5 liters and Ford had nothing in its American line that could relate to such a small capacity. On GT racing the question was: What would happen if Ford competed at Le Mans with some of their own cars homologated in the GT category?

The talks ended abruptly after ten days of negotiations. Frey received a telephone call from one of Ferrari's lawyers who told him that there would be no further discussion and the deal was off. The reasons were not made public but Ferrari must have realized the step he was about to make would end the individualistic image that he had created and he could not very well have his cake and eat it too.

After the breakdown of negotiations with Ferrari several other companies were considered, Maserati in Italy, Aston-Martin, Brabham, and Cooper in England among others. Each was rejected for one reason or another and it was decided to establish Ford's own organization in England. The services of John Wyer, former racing manager and general manager of Aston-Martin, were acquired, Ford Advanced Vehicles was formed, and an arrangement was made with Eric Broadley and his Lola Company to use their resources and facilities for one year. Broadley already had some experience with

a midship configuration and had in fact built a Ford-engined prototype. In forming this alliance Ford was able to use this prototype for
the installation and development of the Ford suspension and driveline components.

In 1962 a group from Ford Product Research and Styling areas,
headed by Roy Lunn, had designed, constructed, and developed
the Mustang I sports car. These same personnel were then assigned

*October 6, 1962. The Mustang I, an experimental sports car devel-
oped by Ford Motor Company engineers, was first shown to the
public. The information acquired in the Mustang I study was the
starting point for the development of the original Ford GT-40 concept.
(Ford Motor Co.)*

to the GT program, and the information which evolved from the Mustang I study served as the starting point for concept work on the GT car.

The design and performance objectives for the Ford GT project were largely established by the status of the leading competition. It was evident, from an analysis of the competitors in 1963, that top speeds in excess of 200 mph, average laps of more than 130 mph, and durability to sustain an average of more than 120 mph for 24 hours would be necessary to compete successfully at Le Mans in the ensuing years.

The racing objectives were also established. They required the cars to be potential winners in the long-distance races such as Daytona, Sebring, Spa, Nurburgring, Targa Florio, as well as Le Mans, and to be capable of winning the FIA World Championship for this type of vehicle. Added to these targets was the timing objective that required the cars to be racing within one year of starting the ambitious program.

Attempting to meet these objectives was a tremendous technical challenge, particularly starting from scratch; whereas, competition had reached its sophisticated product level after many years of evolutionary development. It was therefore considered necessary to pursue a highly analytical approach to the design in its concept stage rather than rely on evolutionary development. The magnitude of the engineering problems involved may be better appreciated by a look at the conditions that exist on a race track such as Le Mans. The accompanying diagram shows this famous circuit, which is made up of conventional roads that are closed to commercial traffic only for the race in June and a short practice session in April. The cars travel clockwise on this 8.3-mile track and encounter road conditions which test every aspect of a car's capabilities. In the 1966 event, speeds

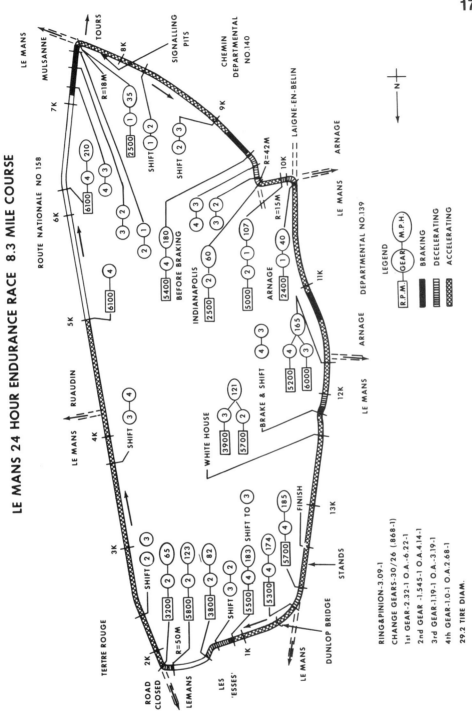

Calculations for the performance of the GT-40 at Le Mans.

ranged from 215 mph on the main straight to 35 mph on the slowest corner, incurring severe braking, acceleration, and constant shifting up and down through the gears. Other corners had to be negotiated at speeds up to 175 mph, and there was full power application for the major part of the circuit. The 24 hours' duration of the race, with its night-day aspect and varied weather conditions, necessitated a fully equipped road vehicle in every sense. For reference against the original objectives, the 1966 event was won at an average speed of 126 mph, despite considerable rain, and a new lap record was set at over 142 mph.

The initial problem was to select a vehicle configuration which was likely to meet the performance objectives and could be packaged within the FIA rule limitations. The Mustang I exercise had clearly shown the advantages of using midship engine configuration to attain a low sleek vehicle silhouette. This arrangement also offered excellent weight distribution characteristics and had been well proved in other spheres of racing, such as Formula 1. It was therefore decided to pursue this same configuration in the GT car.

Initial package studies showed that the essential components could be installed in a vehicle silhouette of 156 inches long, 40 inches high (hence the name GT 40), and 95-inch wheelbase, and still meet the FIA requirements. The overall arrangement included a forward hinged canopy top; twin radiators, located behind the seats with side-ducting; the 256 CID V-8 engine developed for Indianapolis; cross-over tuned exhausts; forward-located spare wheel, oil tank, and battery; fixed seats and movable controls; side-sill gas tanks; and, because no suitable transaxle existed within the company, a proprietary vendor-developed unit was selected, this unit being manu-factured by Colloti in Italy.

Concurrently with package development, a full-sized clay model

Outline packages showing the evolution of the GT-40 from the experimental Mustang I. The lower outline is of the later development MK II.

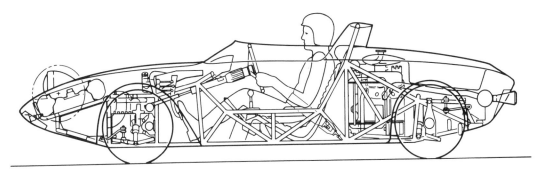

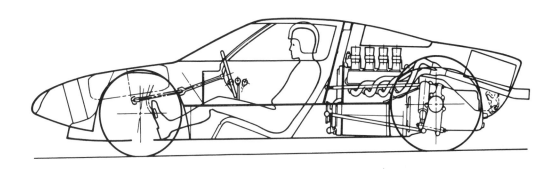

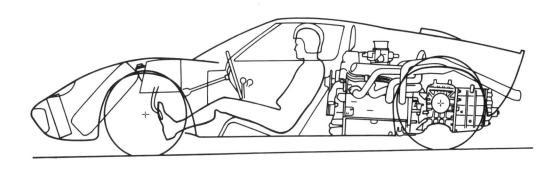

was constructed for overall shape appraisal. The essential requirement was to encompass the basic mechanical ingredients and meet the FIA rule limitations. With these exceptions, however, the choice of shape was largely determined by what seemed right at the time, as there was no previous knowledge of road car forms developed for speeds in excess of 200 mph.

Subsequent analysis of side radiators showed heat dissipation to be marginal, and a forward-located unit was therefore adopted. The hinged canopy was dropped in favor of two separate doors in order to meet the FIA rule requirements clearly.

Having arrived at the basic configuration and initial shape, an analysis program was planned for the following areas: (1) aerodynamics; (2) engine; (3) transaxle-driveshafts; (4) body; (5) suspension, steering, brakes, and wheels; (6) interior-driver environment; and (8) fuel system.

AERODYNAMICS

It was evident from the outset of the project that aerodynamics would play a major part in the program. With the exception of land-speed record cars, no vehicle had been developed to travel at speeds in excess of 200 mph on normal highways. The speeds involved were greater than the takeoff speed of most aircraft, but, conversely, the main problem was to keep the vehicle on the ground.

Following initial package and shape studies, a ⅜ aerodynamic model was constructed, and a series of tests were carried out at the University of Maryland wind tunnel. Early tests showed that, although the drag factor was satisfactory, the lift at 200 mph was over half the weight of the vehicle. Subsequent tests with variations of nose height showed the low nose to have some advantage, but lifts were still totally unacceptable. The major improvement came with the addition of "spoilers" under the front end, which not only reduced the lift to an acceptable standard, but, quite surprisingly, also reduced drag.

With the basic car and no spoiler, drag was 503 pounds and front axle lift 528 pounds. With the high nose shape the drag increased to 519 pounds and front axle lift was 519 pounds. With the low nose shape drag was reduced to 507 pounds and front lift to 445 pounds and with a 3.50 deep spoiler and the low nose configuration, drag dropped to 488 pounds and front end lift to a figure of 236 pounds.

It should be remembered that the tests were conducted with a $\frac{3}{8}$ model with equivalent speed readings of 128 mph. Results, therefore, had to be extrapolated to 200 mph, and ground effects could not be recorded. Shown in the diagram are the total drag and rolling resistance curves plotted against available horsepower. This shows that the car should reach approximately 210 mph. In actual fact, the original GT 40's could only reach 197 mph in still air, although they did exceed 200 mph when passing other cars. The reason for this discrepancy was established when the actual prototype was tested in a full-sized wind tunnel. It was found that 76 of the 350 horsepower available were being absorbed in internal ducting such as radiators, brake ducts, engine air, and interior ventilation, whereas only 30 hp had been allowed for these items in the original calculations. Another item which did not show up in these early wind tunnel tests was the aerostability problem, which is discussed later in this chapter.

ENGINE

As previously mentioned, the engine selected for the GT 40 was the 4.2-liter (256 CID) unit that had been developed by Ford Motor

Company for the 1963 Indianapolis race. It was derived from the 289 Fairlane engine but included the use of aluminum block and heads and a dry sump oil system, but, unlike the Ford double overhead camshaft Indianapolis engine, still retained push rods. To adapt these units for road racing required detuning to run on commercial pump fuel; addition of full-sized alternator and starter systems; changes to the scavenge system for greater variations of speed and cornering; providing an induction system with greater flexibility for road use in adverse climatic conditions; and general detail changes to suit the package installation. These engines gave approximately 350 hp in their detuned state for long-distance races.

TRANSAXLE DRIVESHAFTS

The vendor-developed Colloti transaxle was packaged into the concept despite its disadvantages of having only four speeds and nonsynchromesh engagement. This unit had been used previously on lightweight vehicles in sprint events, but analysis showed that it should be capable of handling the GT 40 power requirements. In addition, it was the only commercially available unit that would meet the timing objectives. The driveshafts were originally planned with single Cardan universal joints at the outboard end and pot joints inboard. Rubber couplings were later selected for the inboard end, mainly in an attempt to dampen out harshness and improve general driveline durability.

BODY

It was elected to use a thin sheet steel (.024 inch–.028 inch) construction to avoid lengthy development of exotic lightweight materials. The strength-carrying structure consisted of a unitized underbody with torque box side sills to house the fuel cells, two main bulkheads, a roof section, and end structures to pick up the suspension mountings. Front and rear substructures were attached to provide for body support, spare wheel, radiator, and battery mountings, and to give supports for the quick lifting jacks. The doors were cut extensively into the roof to provide reasonable entry and exit and, together with end sections and rocker panels, were made of hand-laminated fiberglass materials. Great care was taken to design all fittings flush with the body panels, including the glass sections which were installed by adhesive techniques. The use of steel sheet for the structure allowed normal methods of welding and brazing in the fabrication. Projection welding was used extensively because of the many blind sections in the structural members. The resulting structure provided an extremely strong unit, giving over 10,000 ft/lb per degree in torsional rigidity.

SUSPENSION, STEERING, BRAKES, AND WHEELS

A number of factors governed design of the suspension units. The package size imposed space limitations; the lightweight structure required spreading the attachment points to minimize point loadings; the high-speed aerodynamic tests indicated the desirability of "anti" features; these units required adjustability to suit the varying circuits; and the resulting balance of compromise still had to provide for excellent road-handling characteristics.

The front suspension was designed as a double "A" frame, with cast-magnesium upright supporting the live wheel spindle and the Girling aluminum brake caliper. The foot well and the position of the spare wheel necessitated an unusually short top arm. The support axes of the "A" frames were arranged to provide an antidive feature of approximately 30 percent. The rear suspension used double-trailing links from the main bulkhead and transverse links comprising a top strut and inverted lower "A" frame. The angling of the "A" frames to the magnesium upright casting, combined with the arrangement of linkage geometry, provided antilift and antisquat features of approximately 30 percent.

These multilink suspensions presented a problem in establishing wheel geometry. Extensive use of the computer was required with so many links moving in different planes and on canted axes. Once the basic configuration of suspension linkage had been established, a computer program was formulated that took into account all the factors involved. Curves could then be plotted in a matter of a few hours to meet a given condition—a process which speeded up the design period and aided the balance of compromise involved.

A rack and pinion was selected for the steering system, mainly because it was particularly suitable for the package conditions involved. The rack had a ratio of 16:1, which in turn gave an overall ratio of $2\frac{1}{2}$ turns of the steering wheel from lock to lock. Girling CR and BR racing calipers were used front and rear, respectively, with solid cast-iron discs, which were $11\frac{1}{2}$ x $\frac{1}{2}$ inches thick. A dual master cylinder was employed for separate front and rear braking systems which incorporate a balance mechanism for adjustment of braking distribution.

Cast-magnesium wheels were originally specified, but development problems precluded their use on the first cars. Prototypes were therefore fitted with wire wheels with alloy rims of 15-inch diameter with a $6\frac{1}{2}$-inch-wide front rim and an 8-inch-wide rear rim.

INTERIOR-DRIVER ENVIRONMENT

Driver environment was a major consideration as long-distance races require maximum driver concentration for periods of up to four hours. An interior buck was constructed as a physical aid in developing seating conditions and to determine optimum positioning of instrumentation and controls. The fixed-seat, movable pedal concept was carried over from the Mustang I project. This arrangement offered structural advantages and provided snug support around the driver to help prevent fatigue from high-speed cornering effects. A nylon netting was used for the basic support medium and was covered with a pad containing ventilation holes to help evaporate driver perspiration. The pedals were mounted on a cast-alloy member which could be adjusted for variation in driver size.

Instruments were positioned so that their faces pointed directly at the driver in order to minimize distortions and reflections. All switches and controls were located and formed so that they could be reached easily and recognized visually or by touch. Flow-through ventilation was provided, together with full protection from adverse weather conditions.

FUEL SYSTEM

To contain the allowable 42 gallons of fuel in this small package, provide for rapid filling, devise a means of picking up the fuel, and provide adequate driver safety was a study within itself. The arrangement selected was two separate tank systems in the side sills, each with its own filler cap and fuel pickup box. These separate systems were designed with individual electric pumps feeding a common supply pipe to the carburetors. Provision was also made in one tank for a reserve pickup unit. The steel shell of the tanks was, of course, part of the main structure. In these were fitted neoprene bags to aid in crash safety. Baffling was attained by means of a plate supported from the top inspection cover.

THE PROTOTYPE

The design and analytical studies were completed during the summer of 1963, together with a clay model reflecting the package changes. The problem was then how and where to execute the final design build and development.

It was finally decided to complete this phase of the program in Europe, since many of the proprietary components were readily available in this area, as were experienced craftsmen in this field of racing. In September, 1963, the center of activity was therefore moved from Dearborn to England, together with a nucleus of Ford engineers, designer's car layouts, power-pack components, and full-sized models.

Component testing was completed by the end of November, 1963, and the remainder of that winter was spent in detailing and procuring items for the building of the first prototypes. The first GT 40 car was completed on April 1, 1964, some eleven months after putting pencil to paper in Dearborn. A second vehicle was completed ten days later, and hectic preparations were made to get both vehicles to the Le Mans practice on April 16. Bad weather conditions in England prevented any serious testing and the cars had an aggregate of only four hours' running time with no high-speed experience before being shipped to France. The first day of practice was rain-drenched, and after very few laps the first car was totally wrecked on the Mulsanne Straight when it left the road at over 150 mph. The second vehicle also experienced trouble and suffered a minor collision. Luckily, both drivers were unharmed, but obviously some stability phenomenon existed that had not been apparent during the design analytical phase. The problem and the solution were found within one week after returning to England, where further testing was carried out at the MIRA proving ground. The fault was

April 1, 1964. The first Ford GT-40 prototype designed for world endurance racing was completed in 11 months after Ford engineers put pencil to paper in Dearborn, Michigan. Like the Mustang I, it employed midship engine configuration. (Ford Motor Co.)

found to have been an aerostability condition which caused rotary motion of the rear end of the vehicle, comparable to that of an arrow without feathers. The motion had increased with speed and, accentuated by the wet track, eventually resulted in rear-end breakaway. Subsequently it was found that the adaptation of a rear-end "spoiler" not only had the effect of putting feathers on an arrow, but also slightly reduced drag, as was previously mentioned. Apparently the spoiler created an airtail which artificially increased the vehicle's aspect ratio and moved the pressure rearward. It also increased the adhesion of the rear wheels and, surprisingly, the effect of this small addition could be felt down to 70 mph.

The second car from the Le Mans practice was modified by the addition of the spoiler and was rebuilt in readiness for the GT 40's first race outing at the Nurburgring on May 31, 1964. The car performed most favorably in practice and qualified second only to the fastest Ferrari. It also ran second in this 1,000-kilometer race in the early hours, but retired after 2½ hours. The reason for the retirement was a suspension-bracket failure because of an incorrect welding process, but when the vehicle was examined, there were several other areas showing stress and near failure. The outing was therefore most successful as a development exercise, and the lessons learned were quickly incorporated in the three vehicles being built for the Le Mans race in mid-June, 1964.

These vehicles were completed and weighed in at the Le Mans scrutineering at 1,960 pounds, less driver and fuel. In practice, the cars qualified second, fourth, and ninth. During the race, one car held the lead for the early hours before retiring with a transmission failure. The second car retired after five hours with a broken fuel line, and the third car retired after 13½ hours with transaxle problems but not before establishing an all-time lap record.

Every attempt was made to correct the transaxle problems within the limited time available before the next race at Reims, France, on July 5, 1964. Again, the cars led the race in the early hours, set new lap records, but all retired with transaxle failures. In addition, the nature of the circuit showed insufficient cooling of the brake discs which remained red hot during the entire time the cars were running.

June, 1964. Ford's first try at Le Mans with the GT-40 met with failure. Three cars were entered. One led for 35 laps before retiring with transmission failure. The second retired after 5 hours, and the third after 13¹/₂ hours. The GT-40 set a new lap and top-speed record. (Ford Motor Co.)

February 28, 1965. First victory. Ford's first big win in world endurance racing came at Daytona Beach. The GT-40 finished first and third, setting an average speed record of 99.9 mph for the 2,000 kilometers. (Ford Motor Co.)

THE EVOLUTION OF FORD MOTOR ·CO

1962	
1963	**MUSTANG II** EXPERIMENTAL SPORTS
1964	**MUSTANG** FORD DIVISION PRODUCTION VEHICLE
1965	
1966	**MACH I** EXPERIMENTAL SPORTS
1967	**MACH II** EXPERIMENTAL SPORTS **FORD MARK III** LIMITED PRODUCTION STREET VEHICLE

XPERIMENTAL AND SPORTS PROTOTYPE VEHICLES

MUSTANG I
EXPERIMENTAL SPORTS

FORD MARK I GT-40
F.I.A. GT PROTOTYPE

FORD MARK I-A GT-40
F.I.A. GT PROTOTYPE

FORD MARK II
F.I.A. SPORTS PROTOTYPE

FORD X-I
EXPERIMENTAL MODIFIED SPORTS

FORD GT-40
F.I.A. PRODUCTION SPORTS

FORD MARK II-A
F.I.A. SPORTS PROTOTYPE

FORD "J" CAR
EXPERIMENTAL SPORTS PROTOTYPE

MIRAGE
J.W. ENGINEERING F.I.A. SPORTS PROTOTYPE

FORD MARK II-B
F.I.A. SPORTS PROTOTYPE

FORD MARK IV
F.I.A. SPORTS PROTOTYPE

The GT 40's first season of racing in 1964, therefore, showed seven starts in major events with no finishes. The cars demonstrated that they met the performance objectives but failed badly on durability aspects.

The winter of 1964 was devoted to detail preparation of the cars for the 1965 season, and at this stage the responsibility for racing the vehicles was given to the Shelby-American racing team. Twenty-

1966. Ford captured the World Manufacturers Championship for production sports cars. Following the 1965 season, 50 MK I vehicles were built to qualify them for the F.I.A. production sports car category. In the hands of private race teams, the cars won the world championship without difficulty. (Ford Motor Co.)

one modifications were executed on the transaxles, the rubber drive-shafts were replaced with Dana couplings, and the decision was made to install standard 289 CID cast-iron engines, using wet sump lubrication. The original cast wheels were also installed and increased to 8-inch front and 9½-inch rear rims. Two of these cars made their first appearance in the 1965 season at the Daytona 2,000 kilometer race on February 28, 1965. They finished first and third in this event, setting an average speed record of 99.9 mph for the distance in 12 hr. 20 min.

Two vehicles also were entered in the Sebring race in March, 1965, and finished second overall and first in class, once more demonstrating that a fair degree of durability had been attained. These cars were raced by the company once more in 1965 at Le Mans, but without success.

The decision was then made to manufacture 50 of these cars in order to qualify them for the production sports car category. These cars were completed in the 1965 period after details changes and the adoption of the 5-speed ZF transaxle. These GT 40's were sold to the public and, in the hands of private race teams and individuals, won the FIA World Championship for production sports cars in 1966.

CHAPTER **8**

The Mark II, J-Car, and Mark IV

In the fall of 1964 the engineering team, headed by Roy Lunn, relocated in Dearborn and started operations at Kar-Kraft, a Ford-contracted facility. This team continued engineering the GT 40 and also started a new experimental vehicle project.

The 1964 season had shown the prototype GT 40's were currently competitive on performance factors but lacked durability. Although work was progressing on correcting durability problems, it was obvious that the GT 40 performance in the fast-moving racing field would soon be outmoded. The problem was how to get an improved power-to-weight factor and at the same time achieve a high durability level. The alternatives were to generate more power from the 289 CID series engine or adapt the 427 CID engine which had been developed for stock-car racing. This latter approach would also involve the development of a unique transaxle to handle the higher power. The other indeterminates were whether the additional weight (some 250 pounds) for the larger engine and heavier transaxle and driveline would unduly deteriorate handling and accentuate braking problems. It was decided, however, to explore this approach by constructing a test vehicle and physically evaluating its performance. The program was initiated in the winter of 1964 and was designated the Mark II project. At the outset, it should be emphasized that the exercise was intended to generate information for a future model, and there was no intention of racing the car.

Package studies showed the 427 CID engine could be accommodated in the GT 40 basic structure by modifying the seating position and rear bulkhead members. The basic suspension units were unchanged, but provision was made for 8-inch-wide cast magnesium front wheels and 9½-inch rear wheels. Housing of the wider spare wheel necessitated revising its position, and the new front-end arrangement made provisions for a remote engine oil tank on the bulkhead and a larger radiator.

A major problem was to generate a transaxle unit which would handle the 427 CID power and the extra weight of the vehicle. For expediency the gear cluster from the conventional 427 CID driveline was used but with completely new housings and axle unit. This approach resulted in a heavier and less efficient arrangement than a direct transfer box, but had the advantage of using developed components. The housings were designed in magnesium, and a pair of quick-change gears transmitted the power to the pinion shaft. The resulting overall package from these changes required new front and rear structures and body shells.

The first experimental MK II was completed during April, 1965, and was evaluated on the 5-mile oval at Ford's Michigan proving ground. After only a few hours of tailoring, the car lapped this circuit at an average speed of 201½ mph and exceeded 210

April, 1965. The first experimental MK II vehicle, built around the Ford 7-liter (427 cu. in.) V-8 engine, was completed by the then new Kar-Kraft facility. They set new lap and top-speed records at Le Mans before retiring with transmission and clutch troubles. (Ford Motor Co.)

October, 1965. The Ford X-1 modified sports car was unveiled. It was a lightweight open-cockpit version of the Ford Mark II. It looked promising but ran in a few races for modified sports cars with no real success. (Ford Motor Co.)

mph on the straightaway. Subsequent testing on road circuits showed that handling had deteriorated only slightly. From the results of these tests, it was calculated that this vehicle should be capable of lapping the Le Mans circuit in from 3 min. 30 sec. to 3 min. 35 sec. without exceeding 6,200 rpm. If these lap times could be realized at this relatively low engine revolutions per minute, the car would obviously have high potential to win at Le Mans. It was decided, therefore, to attempt to run two of these experimental cars in the

The MK II's were fitted with fins to improve stability at the 1965 Le Mans race. (Ford Motor Co.)

1965 Le Mans event as an exploratory exercise. This decision was made at the end of April, and the cars went to the event without the benefit of the practice Le Mans weekend.

In the ensuing five weeks the first car underwent initial testing and rebuilding, and a second car was hurriedly constructed. The second actually arrived at Le Mans without even having turned a wheel. Since the April workout was missed, the first evening of prerace practice was spent in tailoring the cars to the circuit. On the

The MK II Le Mans car on test. (Ford Motor Co.)

second evening the car that had never run before arriving at the track set an all-time record lap of 3 min. 33 sec., an average speed of 141 mph.

One car qualified first and when the race started on Saturday, both cars went out ahead of the field and comfortably lapped at 3 min. 40 sec. without exceeding 6,000 rpm. Unfortunately, hurried preparation resulted in the cars being retired after two and seven hours, respectively, with nonfundamental driveline problems. One car had a speck of sand in the clutch slave cylinder, which caused the piston to stick and generate heat at the throw-out bearing. The heat, in turn, softened an oil-retaining ring in the axle, ultimately resulting in loss of oil. The second car broke a gear which had been incorrectly drilled. The cars, however, achieved their purpose of establishing the capability of the engine-driveline combination. The potential indicated in this initial experimental outing resulted in the 1966 program being based on the MK II vehicle.

The following chart shows the MK II power-to-weight factor compared to the original GT 40 and the production version. Vehicle weights are quoted, less fuel and driver.

TYPE	VEHICLE WEIGHT	HP	HP/LB.
MK II	2,400 lbs.	485	0.202
Production GT 40	2,150 lbs.	385	0.179
Prototype GT 40	1,960 lbs.	350	0.179

After it was apparent that the 7-liter pushrod engine was going to be used, Jacques Passino, manager of Special Vehicles Activity, and Carroll Shelby asked for all possible weight reduction in the

Engine compartment and rear suspension of the MK II. (Ford Motor Co.)

Gearbox of the MK II. (Ford Motor Co.)

engine. Gus Scussel, then engineer at Ford's Engine and Foundry division, was in charge of the project and achieved the results with aluminum heads, an aluminum hub on the vibration damper, and a water pump of the same alloy, reducing it from the 602 pounds of the NASCAR version to 550 pounds, these being dry weights less exhaust manifold, air cleaner, and clutch. Scussel was confident from the outset that the engine had the durability to go 24 hours, providing the revolutions per minute range could be controlled. All that was needed was refinement, and to keep the speed range to where Scussel wanted it. Orders were given to all drivers that 6,200 rpm was the limit. No exceptions, even though the engine had a safe limit of 7,400 rpm for short-term use. To this end, each car's tachometer was accurately calibrated and a calibration chart taped in the driver's side-door jamb.

Aluminum heads meant a small reduction in valve size from the NASCAR version; gauge diameter of intakes was reduced from 2.16 to 2.06 inches; exhausts from 1.70 to 1.625 inches. Otherwise head design remained the same, but compression ratio was reduced from 12.5:1 to 10.5:1 because Le Mans fuel is only 101 octane compared to the 102.8 permitted in stock-car racing. As far as octane requirement is concerned, the 10.5:1 aluminum head is about equivalent to a 10.0:1 iron head because it conducts the heat away faster. The regular "hiriser" intake manifold was retained.

Aside from the aluminum heads, the most important change for GT use was a dry sump. This was completely redesigned by Engine and Foundry and had two scavenge pumps driven by an internal chain from the crankshaft, replacing the previous pump driven by an external, toothed belt. The pressure pump was gear-driven from the camshaft and produced 65–70 psi at 6,000 rpm. The oil cooler was a NASCAR item and was so effective that in cold weather it was necessary to blank off parts of the cooler. Maximum oil temperature under any conditions encountered was 250°F.

Tailoring the engine for the GT also included devising a suitable exhaust system and carburetion. With the exhaust it was simply a matter of getting the required length of pipe for every cylinder and fitting the resulting bundle into the small space available. Somewhat surprisingly, the carburetion settled upon was a single 4-barrel Holley unit, rated at 780 cu. ft./min. flow. This looks old among the multiple Webers of competing cars, but proved completely suitable. Engine and Foundry wanted vacuum-operated secondary throttle opening, but tester Ken Miles won out and mechanical opening was fitted. This was accomplished by a cam-and-rod arrangement designed for equal opening, primary and secondary.

Durability testing was in the usual thorough Ford way. Ford

dynamometer facilities were extensive and comprehensive, able to duplicate accurately any driving pattern through computer-programmed changes of speed, load, and throttle opening. After preliminary test runs by drivers in an elaborately instrumented car (measuring and recording on oscillograph such things as engine speed, manifold vacuum, rear-wheel speed, throttle plate angle, and axle shaft torque), it was comparatively simple for Ford dynamometer people to reproduce the track conditions on an engine test stand. The dynamometer cycle allowed 6,800 rpm in first and second gear, 6,250 in third and top, and was run for 48 hours, as compared to the 6,200 limit for drivers and about 38 hours normally put on a given engine (4-hour break-in, 4-hour vehicle sort-out, 6-hour practice, 24-hour race). Thus at race time durability was a known factor.

In preparation for 1966, a concentrated vehicle development program was planned using the Daytona, Sebring, and Riverside tracks. In addition, specialized component developments were initiated on items such as engine, ignition and electrical system, transaxle, driveshafts and brakes. Although some fundamental changes emerged from this development program, the main emphasis was on refinement to establish durability rather than improve performance.

Major changes that resulted from testing and development included: (1) New shorter nose configuration to save weight and improve aerodynamics; (2) addition of external rear-brake scoops; (3) higher efficiency radiators; (4) strengthened chassis brackets; (5) live rear hubs for improved durability; (6) internal scavenge pump to minimize vulnerability and save weight; (7) generally improved ducting to radiators, carburetors, and brakes; (8) crossover fuel system with single-filler neck; (9) ventilated disc brakes to improve durability; and (10) quick change brake discs designed to facilitate changes during pit stops.

February 6, 1966. The Ford Mark II gained its first victory in the 24-Hour Daytona Continental, as Lloyd Ruby and Ken Miles averaged 109 mph. Mark II cars virtually led all the way and finished 1-2-3. The victory came after almost a year of development work. (Ford Motor Co.)

All these changes were incorporated in the vehicles that made thier first appearance at the Daytona 24-Hour Race on February 5–6, 1966. The MK II cars virtually led the race all the way with a 1-2-3 finish; the complete story of this is told in Chapter 9.

During 1965, while the MK II was being developed, Roy Lunn sketched out some ideas for a successor to the already potent 7 liter. The guidelines called for a car that would be in the 200-mph-plus

The original sketches for the J-Car design. (Ford Motor Co.)

category; it would have to be aerodynamically perfect and yet fit the Appendix J rules of international racing and as such it should dominate the long ultrahigh-speed events. In early October, 1965, armed with a rough profile drawing and certain figures, Lunn approached Gene Bordinat, Ford Motor Company's vice-president and director of styling, and requested that the Styling Office develop such a car to be initially known as GT-P, but later renamed the J-car because it was built to Appendix J specifications.

March 26, 1966. An open-cockpit Ford Mark II sports prototype, driven by Miles and Ruby, won the Sebring 12-Hour race. (Ford Motor Co.)

The MK II Ford prepared for the 1966 season opening race at Daytona Beach, Florida. (Ford Motor Co.)

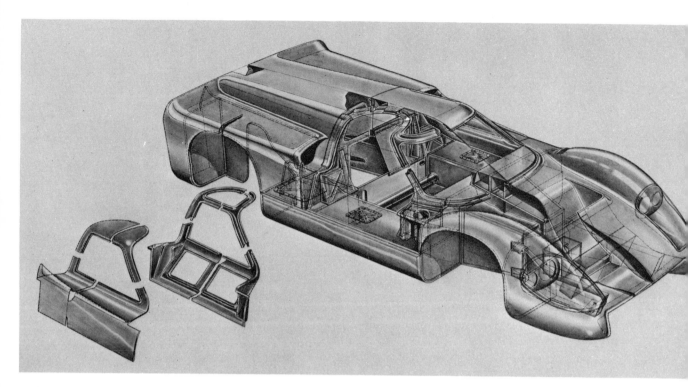

Unitized honeycomb-chassis design of the J-Car. (Ford Motor Co.)

Bordinat assigned the task to the Corporate Projects Studio, which tackled it in an atmosphere of secrecy unusual even in the security-conscious automotive industry.

A handpicked team of stylists, product engineering designers, styling engineers, and clay modelers went about their work in a locked basement room on the door of which was posted the names of those permitted access in the early stages.

The drawing with which the project was launched showed a low frontal area, a chopped-off rear end, and an engine mounted behind the driver with a canopy-covered cockpit.

Original specifications envisioned a 95-inch wheelbase, front and rear tread measuring 54.6 and 53.8 inches, respectively, an overall length of 163.9 inches, a 38.5-inch overall height and a 67.3-inch overall width, 36 inches of front overhand and a 32.9-inch rear overhang. The profile drawing contained no surface detail, but did include some chassis assumptions, including a floor, gas tanks, front and rear bulkheads, and certain other chassis parts constructed of lightweight aluminum honeycomb panels like those used widely in the aircraft industry.

An inch thick in the bulkheads and a half-inch thick in most other areas, the panels consisted of an aluminum core sandwiched between sheets of aluminum less than .020 of an inch thick.

Working on the clay model of the J-Car at Corporate Projects Studio. (Ford Motor Co.)

The completed model of the J-Car. (Ford Motor Co.)

A drawing of a steel armature and a modeling buck specially designed to allow for the car's 4-inch ground clearance was completed by mid-October, and the fabricating shops in the Styling Center set about building them. At the same period a full-scale modeling table on rollers was also made.

Within three days of delivery of the buck, the general shape of the car became apparent. As further progress was made the model was checked constantly to ensure compliance with the rules of the FIA Appendix J.

By December 6 the clay model was far enough along to have molds made of the glass areas so that windshields and side glass could be ordered. Corning Glass had the female molds within a week.

Although some surface refinement remained to be done at this stage, the clay was slicked, Di-Noc was applied, and the model was taken briefly from the Corporate Projects Studio and shown to a group attending the Ford Motorsport Banquet in the Styling Center. It was then returned to the studio for further work.

Early in January a styling project engineer assigned to the program completed the perspective drawing that served thereafter as a "reference document to assure that all parties were talking the same language."

Working closely with Roy Lunn's Kar-Kraft, of Dearborn, which was responsible for final building, Corporate Projects personnel designed a number of structural members and inner panels three dimensionally in clay, from which models were made, and the parts then were either cast in fiberglass or fabricated in metal. This unique approach cut months from the program by eliminating the need for complicated layout drawings and elaborate mahogany die models.

Plaster hammer forms of exterior door and roof panels went to

Troutman-Barnes in California for the buildup of both inner and outer door and roof panels in aluminum.

At this point the Ford stylists hedged their bet. While Troutman-Barnes was doing its work, Ford fabricating services specialists were making the same panels of thin-shell fiberglass in a search for parts lighter in weight than any ever before produced in the company's styling shops.

The search paid off. The fiberglass assemblies proved to be as light as those made of aluminum and the prototype had those styling-fabricated parts—seats, hood, door assemblies, front end, rear canopy, and rear end.

The only visible parts of the car not made in the styling center were the exposed gas tanks on each side of the driver's compartment, and the tires, wheels, and instrument panel.

Racing driver Bruce McLaren was consulted on seating configuration. The shell-like, perforated fiberglass seats were designed specifically to his body contours but were tested with other individuals as well. They were patterned after the seats used in spacecraft.

It was planned at one point to provide rear vision by means of mirrors, mounted on the front quarters, which the driver could see by looking directly through cutouts in the inner door panels. This idea eventually was abandoned, however, in favor of a single, wide-vision, hooded prismatic mirror in the front of the roof.

The engine used for the car was the 7-liter (427 cu. in.) Ford V-8 engine with a bore and stroke of 4.24 $\times$ 3.78 in. With a Holley 4V 7,800 cfm downdraft carburetor, the engine gave 475 bhp at 6,200 rpm. Transmission was by means of a two-speed torque converter and planetary gearbox.

Suspension at the front was by means of two unequal length

arms, coil springs, telescopic shock absorbers, antidive geometry, and antiroll bar. At the rear, suspension was by means of double trailing arms, single transverse top-link lower "A" arm, springs, telescopic shock absorbers, antilift and antisquat geometry, and an antiroll bar.

The 15-inch cast-magnesium wheels were used with 13-inch rim size front and 12.0-inch rim size rear. Dual line hydraulic brakes were fitted with four wheel discs and calipers. The discs were Ford ventilated rotor 11.5-inch diameter types with Girling calipers.

The styling team responsible for the J-Car, with the finished product.
(Ford Motor Co.)

*April, 1966. The Ford J-Car, an experimental vehicle designed to suc-
ceed the Ford Mark II, made its first appearance at the Le Mans trials.
Subsequent tests showed the car was not ready to race and none
were entered in the 24-hour race.* (Ford Motor Co.)

*June 19, 1966. Three years of effort were climaxed at Le Mans when
the Ford Mark II sports prototype, driven by Bruce McLaren and
Chris Amon, rolled across the finish line to capture the first American
victory in the history of the classic endurance test.* (Ford Motor Co.)

August, 1966. A highly modified lightweight version of the J-Car was tested at Riverside Raceway in California. The test ended in tragedy when veteran driver Ken Miles lost his life in a crash, the cause of which still remains a mystery. (Ford Motor Co.)

January, 1967. A second revision of the J-Car was tested at Daytona International Speedway. This test proved the increased chassis rigidity and weight savings offered by the chassis design. The original body configuration was finally rejected because of aerodynamic problems. (Ford Motor Co.)

The car was extensively tested and appeared at the Le Mans, 1966, test weekend but was in fact never raced as the J-Car. Aerodynamics were its main problem and for the 1967 Sebring race a completely revamped version of the J-Car appeared with the new name Mark IV.

At the instigation of Shelby-American's Phil Remington, radical changes were made to the front and rear body panels, although the center section remained unchanged. The MK IV turned out to be faster and more stable (straight ahead or in yaw condition) than its predecessor.

The engine of the MK IV was identical to the 1967 Daytona MK II engines, except that the tunnel-port heads were aluminum instead of cast iron, saving 80 pounds in weight. With two 4-barrel Holley carburetors, the Ford claim was 530 bhp, which was five more than the 7 liter with the old type Daytona head.

A mechanic adjusts the twin carburetors of the MK IV Ford. (Ford Motor Co.)

The MK IV development of the J-Car won its first race first time out at Sebring in 1967; it was driven by Bruce McLaren (l.) and Mario Andretti (r.). (Ford Motor Co.)

March, 1967. A new aerodynamic body shell, building upon experience gained in testing the first revision of the J-Car, was developed in the weeks before the Sebring 12-Hour race. The new car was known as the Ford MK IV sports prototype. (Ford Motor Co.)

April 1, 1967. The Ford MK IV made an impressive debut in the 12-Hour Sebring race. Driven by Mario Andretti and Bruce McLaren, the MK IV easily won the race at an average of 102.9 mph. (Ford Motor Co.)

April 5, 1967. Results of the MK IV debut were so encouraging that Ford readied four of the sports prototype vehicles for the 1967 24-Hour Le Mans race. The MK IV won this classic in an all-American finish with Foyt and Gurney breaking all records. (Ford Motor Co.)

April 10, 1967. The 1967 edition of the Ford MK II that won the 1966 race was known as the MK IIB. It showed some subtle refinements in the trials and was used as a backup car to the MK IV's. (Ford Motor Co.)

May 1, 1967. The Mirage-Ford sports prototype scored its first victory in the 1,000 Kilometer Championship race at Spa, Belgium. The Mirage was built by J. W. Engineering, formerly Ford Advanced Vehicles of England. It was a modified version of the MK I (GT-40). (Ford Motor Co.)

The new body and crossover exhaust system necessitated relocating the legal "FIA suitcase" receptacles and spare tire.

The MK IV had an interesting feature in the unitized electrical system, with all the important components installed in a plug-in box mounted in the dash.

It is, of course, now history that the MK IV won its first race with no trouble, running the Sebring 12 hours like clockwork. It then went on to win the 24 hours of Le Mans classic in 1967 by a large margin, setting both speed and endurance records. With two American drivers, Dan Gurney and A. J. Foyt driving the Ford, it was a great American victory in the European classic but it was also destined to be the end of the road for the big 7-liter Fords. At the end of the season the FIA ruled that the capacity of prototypes would be limited to 3 liters and the speedy American cars were legislated off the track.

C H A P T E R **9**

The GT's and Prototypes —A Racing Record

The GT Ford made its debut at the 1,000 kilometer race at the Nurburgring on May 31, 1964. Only one car was entered in the hands of Phil Hill and Bruce McLaren. These two faced a full team of Ferraris led by John Surtees.

Surtees shattered the record with a practice lap of 8 min. 57.9 sec., but Phil Hill showed the Ford was competitive with a time of 9 min. 04.7 sec., which was second fastest in practice.

The 9 A.M. start saw Surtees take an immediate lead with the Ferrari, followed by teammate Ludovico Scarfiotti. Close behind came Phil Hill with the Ford GT and Jo Bonnier in the flat 8-cylinder prototype Porsche.

After five laps Surtees had his Ferrari 50 seconds ahead of the second-place Ferrari driven by Graham Hill, with Scarfiotti in the third Ferrari holding down third place ahead of Phil Hill's Ford.

The Ford GT stopped on lap 11 for Hill to hand over to

McLaren, and the New Zealander got away still in fourth place. Three laps later McLaren brought the car in again and pointed to the rear end. Eric Broadley was at hand and inspected the rear suspension, finding the radius rod broken, and the Ford's race was run—but not before it had made a very strong impression.

The 24 hours of Le Mans was held on June 20–21, 1964, and this was the race that Ford had been shooting for. Three of the GT Fords had been entered to run in the prototype class, the drivers being Phil Hill/Bruce McLaren in car No. 10, Richie Ginther/Masten Gregory in car No. 11, and Dick Attwood/Jo Schlesser in car No. 12. John Surtees/Bandini, with the Ferrari, dominated practice again, turning 3 min. 42 sec., a speed of 135.6 mph—more than 6 mph faster than his previous year's record. Ginther, with one of the Fords, was close behind with a time of 3 min. 45.3 sec. and all the drivers were enthusiastic about the speed and handling of the new Fords. At the start it was the Ferraris in the lead. None of the Fords made a good start but Ginther was in sixth place as the field sorted itself out. Attwood's sister car got away reluctantly and Phil Hill's wouldn't even fire up. The 1958/61/62 winner managed to get his engine going at last and made off long after all the others had departed.

When the leaders came by the pits on the first lap the Ferraris were in the first three positions but Ginther had made up ground fast and was moving very quickly into fourth place.

By the end of lap 2 the blue-and-white Ford was in the lead, averaging more than 127 mph and turning times of 190 mph on the Mulsanne Straight.

Ginther held the lead until the first of the pit stops, about an hour and twenty minutes of racing. The Ford took 2 min. 7 sec. to refuel and the Surtees/Bandini Ferrari only 1 min. 28 sec., so the

The MK I (GT-40) at Le Mans in 1964. (Ford Motor Co.)

The GT-40 in its finalized form. (Ford Motor Co.)

Ferrari was in the lead. From then on the factory Ferrari of Surtees and Bandini dominated the race, although the Ginther/Gregory Ford was never far away until the sixth hour when its Colotti gearbox broke.

The Schlesser/Attwood Ford caught fire out of the Mulsanne corner about an hour earlier and just after 5 A.M. the last Ford GT was out with another broken gearbox.

The first confrontation of Ford and Ferrari in 1965 took place at the 2,000 kilometer Daytona Continental Race on February 28. Shelby-American entered two GT 40's driven by Ken Miles/Lloyd Ruby and Bob Bondurant/Richie Ginther.

While the Ferrari opposition was not official from the factory, it nevertheless included John Surtees as number one driver and Ferrari's chief engineer in charge of the mechanical work.

Surtees showed that the Ferrari was the fastest car on the circuit with a time of 2 min. 0.6 sec., an average speed of 113.731 mph, with Bondurant's Ford second fastest at 2 min. 1.8 sec., an average of 112.610 mph, and the Miles/Ruby car third fastest.

To break up the opposition, Gurney brought along a 5.3-liter Ford V-8 modified by Shelby and fitted into an equally modified Lotus 19 chassis.

Surtees' Ferrari took the lead initially but Bondurant dived down the banking to wrest the lead with the Ford GT. Bondurant's effort was short lived as he overshot the first turn and Surtees was back in front. It was another short-lived lead, however, as Gurney with the Lotus-Ford went out in front and stayed there. A blown tire which shattered the battery and subsequent suspension damage put the Ferrari out of the race, and as darkness fell the Gurney/Grant Lotus-Ford had a tremendous lead of five laps only to retire with a holed piston.

This put the two GT 40 Fords into the first two places. When Bondurant came in to hand over the leading GT to Ginther, the engine refused to start and it was 27 minutes before the car rejoined the race in sixth place.

After 12 hours and 40 minutes on the 3.81-mile circuit, the Ford GT came in to its first victory, Miles and Ruby having covered 327 laps. The Bondurant/Ginther GT had worked its way back up to third place but was 9 laps behind the winner. It looked like a promising season for the Ford team.

For the Sebring 12 Hour Race, two GT Fords were entered in the Prototype class, one for Bruce McLaren and Ken Miles, the other for Phil Hill and Richie Ginther. Gurney was present with his pacesetter, the Ford-engined Lotus 19.

The MK I's (GT-40's) first victory was at the 1965 Daytona Beach race. (Shelby-American)

As the flag dropped for the Le Mans start at 10 A.M. on Saturday, March 27, 1965, it was Ginther that led the pack with one of the Ford GT's. Ginther's lead was short-lived as he had to stop at his pits to try and locate brake problems. Attention now focused on the battle between the Lotus powered by Ford of Gurney and the Chaparral powered by Chevrolet of Jim Hall. Miles and McLaren led the prototype class with the GT but the big sports cars were running away from them. Ginther was back in the race, going as fast as he could to make up a lap and a half lost in the pits.

The Chaparral took the lead but used more fuel than the Ford and when it pitted, Gurney established the Lotus-Ford firmly in the lead with Phil Hill now in third place with the GT.

Just after midday Gurney was out with a broken fuel pump drive and the Phil Hill car was out with a broken spring mounting and the Miles/McLaren GT moved up to third.

When a tropical storm broke out late in the afternoon, the McLaren/Miles GT began to make up time quickly as the car was equipped with narrower tread rain tires. The effort was not enough to catch the leading Chaparral but it guaranteed them a sound second place, four laps behind the leader but two laps ahead of the third-place Ferrari.

The 1,000 kilometers of the Nürburgring was held on May 23, 1965, and the Ford entry was split between Ford Advanced Vehicles from England and Shelby-American.

The green FAV Ford was under the direction of John Wyer and was the open GT 40 prototype with a 4.7-liter Ford V-8 engine and ZF gearbox. The Halibrand wheels used in the Targa Florio were replaced by the original Rudge-type wire-spoke wheels. It was driven by Attwood and John Whitmore, and though it started off in fifth place and moved up to third by default, it was never a serious challenger to the Ferraris and finally retired with engine mount breakage.

Shelby-American entered two Ford GT 40 coupes which had undergone a certain amount of modifications and painted blue with a white stripe.

One of the cars had a 5.3-liter Ford V-8 engine, but even with Phil Hill driving, it was no match for the 4-liter Ferrari of Surtees. However, it did hold second place in the opening laps, but was 30 seconds behind the Surtees Ferrari after only three laps. The 5.3-liter car lasted seven laps before a drive shaft broke. This was no great surprise as the larger capacity engine had twisted one in practice.

The second Shelby entry was a similar coupe with the normal 4.7-liter engine. It was driven by Chris Amon in the opening stages, but was running on seven cylinders. Although quite a way back, it held third place, and with the loss of the 5.3-liter car it was decided to switch Phil Hill and McLaren over to the smaller engined car at the refueling stop and to try to get it to run on eight cylinders.

When Amon was given a signal to stop on the next lap he was busy lapping a slower car and did not see the sign, so he went on for lap 16 and ran out of fuel almost in sight of the pits. He pushed the car along the uphill section to the pits and lost a lot of time. Bruce McLaren took over after refueling but was way down on the score-board. In the rush nothing was done about the engine and it continued to run on seven cylinders, with McLaren lapping steadily around 9 min. 43 sec. Suddenly McLaren turned a lap in 9 minutes as the engine went back on eight cylinders by itself. From then on the car ran very well and Phil Hill took over and pushed the car back up the scoreboard to finish eighth overall.

The third Ford entry was from Ford France and was a normal GT 40 coupe with a 4.7-liter engine. It was in 1964 trim with wire wheels and painted white with blue stripes. Driven by Maurice Trintignant and Guy Ligier, it was never in the picture and finally went out with broken engine mounts although the drivers blamed the gear selector, for when the engine dropped slightly and twisted the gearbox they could not select gears. While an eighth place was not a notable achievement, the GT 40 had at least shown it was reliable under hard driving.

For the Targa Florio, a new roadster GT 40 Ford was entered by the John Wyer organization from England. It was driven by Bob Bondurant and John Whitmore and was fitted with a normal 4.7-liter engine.

On the tricky Sicilian road circuit the Ferraris outclassed the lone Ford entry. Nino Vaccarella's Ferrari turned one lap at 39 min. 29 sec. compared to the Ford's fastest lap of 41 min. 46 sec.

On lap 1 the Ford ran third behind the two factory-entered Ferraris, dropping to fourth on lap 2 when it was passed by another privately entered Ferrari.

On lap 3 the Ford GT was back in third place as one of the leading Ferraris had crashed, but the Ford's rear tires were wearing out every two laps.

Just after Whitmore took over from Bondurant, the hub cap detached itself from the center-lock front wheel and the wheel came off. Fortunately Whitmore managed to come to a halt without hitting anything and recovered the wheel, fitted it back on the hub, and drove slowly to the pits. His efforts were wasted, as Bondurant crashed the car on lap 9.

With the success of the tests in the USA it was decided to enter two of the 7-liter (427 cu. in.) Ford MK II's for the Le Mans 24 Hour Race. One of these cars was driven by Phil Hill and Chris Amon, the other by Bruce McLaren and Ken Miles. Backing them up were the three GT 40's of Bondurant/Maglioli, Whitmore/ Ireland, and the Ford France car of Trintignant/Ligier.

During the Thursday practice session Surtees' Ferrari unofficially broke the lap record with a time of 3 min. 38.1 sec. and Bondurant surprised everyone when he took the GT 40 around in 3 min. 38.7 sec. for the second fastest time of the day.

There was a special practice session on the evening before the race and Shelby gave Phil Hill the "Go" with the MK II. The result was an astounding 3 min. 33 sec., an average speed of 141.4 mph. When the 51 starters got away at 4 P.M. on June 19, 1965, the two blue-and-white 7-liter Fords streaked into the lead with the factory-entered Ferraris behind them.

Calmly the Fords drew away from the red Italian cars; McLaren breaking the lap record with a time of 3 min. 41.2 sec., which was an indication of how much they had in reserve.

After little more than an hour's racing the two Ford MK II's were in for fuel. Despite a relatively small carburetor they had a consumption of about 4 miles per gallon.

The pit stops gave the Ferrari the lead, but when the two Ferraris also went in to refuel the Fords were back out in front.

Amon took over the car from Phil Hill but his lead did not last very long and the MK II was in the pits for 40 minutes to attend to the gearbox. When the car rejoined the race it was in 35th place.

In the first hour of the race the Ford France GT 40 retired with gearbox failure.

After two hours McLaren still held the lead but could use only top gear and the Ferraris were closing up. One more hour and the leading Ford was out of the race with a broken gearbox. The Bondurant/Maglioli GT 40 was out with a blown head gasket and the Whitemore/Ireland GT 40 retired with overheating problems. Phil Hill, back at the wheel of the MK II, made up ground fast, rocketing through the field from 35th to 6th and setting a new lap record of 3 min. 37.7 sec., an average speed of 138.3 mph, but before midnight the last of the Fords was silent with a broken gearbox. The speed to win was there but the reliability was not.

The first race in the 1966 Manufacturers G. T. Championship was held on the road/track circuit at Daytona Beach, February 5–6. The Continental had been extended to a full 24-hour race with a lineup of 60 cars. For the Daytona event the Ford team was split in two with Shelby-American handling three cars and Holman & Moody handling two. All these factory entries were MK II's, the GT 40's being in private owners hands.

The Shelby-American team was made up of Bruce McLaren/ Chris Amon, Dan Gurney/Jerry Grant, and Ken Miles/Lloyd Ruby. The drivers for the Holman & Moody team were Walt Hansgen/ Mark Donohue and Ron Bucknum/Richie Ginther, the latter entry having a full automatic transmission.

The Ferrari factory was not officially represented but the Ferrari opposition was strong enough in the form of two Type 365P2's from North American Racing Team and another from Ecurie Francorchamps. Other opposition to the Fords was the Chaparral driven by Phil Hill and Jo Bonnier.

In practice the Fords experienced problems of both mechanical and organizational nature. The wider tires used caused them to rub on the bodywork on the banking and cutouts had to be made on the fenders, these later being covered with plexiglass. The Ferrari of Pedro Rodriguez set the pace in practice with a time of 1 min. 59.2 sec., but just before the end of the practice session Ken Miles took his MK II out and turned a lap of 1 min. 57.8 sec., a speed of

116.434 mph to take pole position on the grid. Bonnier with the Chaparral was 0.2 second slower, which gave him second place on the grid. Race day was cold and windy and at 2:30 P.M. the cars lined up for their pace lap.

Bonnier in the Chaparral led on the first lap but Miles was by on lap 2, with Hansgen's Ford in third place trailed by two Ferraris. The pace was so great that the leaders were catching the tail end of the field after only two laps.

Ginther made an early pit stop in the automatic Ford MK II with brake trouble due to a faulty master cylinder. This was repaired but not before they had lost many laps.

When the Chaparral pitted, the Fords were firmly in first and second places followed by a Ferrari and a GT 40 Ford of the Essex Wire team in fourth place.

The lead changed briefly just after 7 P.M. when due to pit stops the Miles/Ruby Ford lost the lead to the Hansgen/Donohue Ford for a period of 7 laps. The GT 40 driven by Bill Wonder retired after having lost a wheel earlier in the race.

Leading the Sports class at dawn were the Essex Wire GT 40's. One car had only fourth and fifth gears left, but with the low torque of the 4.7-liter engine this was not affecting the lap times too much.

With the first daylight pit stops for tire changes, the blanking over the radiators was removed. On McLaren's car they were a little late, as when a mechanic checked the water a geyser shot up covering the car with rust-stained water. McLaren and Amon had been set the slowest lap times of the factory-entered Fords to conserve their car and for this reason they were lying fifth, fifteen laps behind the leader. A retirement at dawn was the Holman & Moody MK II, the automatic transmission having given out after 1,350 miles of hard driving.

Gurney had moved his MK II up into second place, but when Grant took over it was noticed he was not using the lower gears and Gurney admitted he could not engage first and second.

As the sun got higher so the temperature rose rapidly. The Essex Wire GT 40 Ford leading the Sports class suddenly came to the pits with its gearbox split open, while the other car also stopped, the internals of its gearbox having gone completely. One lap short of lap 500, Dan Gurney set a new record of 1 min. 57.7 sec., an average speed of 116.51 mph.

As midday passed and the last fuel and tire changes took place, it was obvious that the Fords were going to score a 1-2-3 victory and so it ended, with Miles and Ruby covering 678 laps at an average speed of 108.02 mph, the Gurney/Grant Ford MK II eight laps behind in second place, Hansgen/Donohue another lap back in third place and the McLaren/Amon MK II in fifth place. It was an encouraging start for the 1966 season.

At Sebring the Ford entry was made up of two cars from Shelby-American and two cars from Holman & Moody. These teams were equipped with the 7-liter MK II cars and were backed up by two more entries from the Alan Mann Racing Team which fielded two special lightweight GT 40's. As these GT 40's were lightened by about 140 pounds, they were not eligible to run in the Sports category and were classed as Prototypes, together with the bigger engined MK II's. Shelby-American nominated Ken Miles/Lloyd Ruby and Dan Gurney/Jerry Grant as drivers, the Holman & Moody cars being driven by Walt Hansgen/Mark Donohue and A. J. Foyt/Ron Bucknum.

The two British entered GT 40's were driven by Graham Hill/Jackie Stewart and John Whitmore/Frank Gardner.

Backing up the six Ford factory cars were two teams of GT 40's

GT-40's were run in Europe in private teams such as the Essex Wire group during 1966. (Robert P. Tronolone)

entered by the Essex Wire Corporation for Revson/Scott and Pabst/Gregory, and the Canadian Comstock Racing Team with Weitzes/Fisher and McLean/Oulette at the wheel. There were three other privately entered Ford GT 40's.

Facing the full for team were two Chaparrals, a P2 Ferrari, and the latest Model P3 Ferrari entered by the Italian factory.

The Miles/Ruby car was an open version of the MK II and was initially fitted with automatic transmission. Troubles with the automatic were experienced during practice and it was replaced with a manual transmission for the race. The Foyt/Bucknum car was also fitted with automatic transmission which was retained for the race.

The three practice sessions on Wednesday, Thursday, and Friday before the race gave plenty of time to sort out the various problems. The first two days of practice were dominated by the performance of the P3 Ferrari, although the Hill/Stewart GT 40 was close behind in times.

On the last day of practice Gurney finally had the MK II sorted out and turned a lap in 2 min. 54.6 sec. (107.22 mph), which was 5 seconds faster than the Chaparral record of the previous year. At the start of the race Graham Hill was away first. Gurney had difficulty in starting his pole position MK II and as a result was in 63d place on lap 1.

The MK II at Le Mans test day 1966. (Ford Motor Co.)

The Ford garage, Le Mans, 1966. (Ford Motor Co.)

Graham Hill came around in the lead on lap 1, closely followed by the P3 Ferrari and the Ferrari Dino. The P3 Ferrari then took the lead but Gurney was making up time fast. He went from 63d on lap 1 to 23d on lap 3 to 10th on lap 8. After an hour and a half of racing, Gurney passed the P3 Ferrari into first place and set about piling up a big lead.

Both the Holman & Moody cars were in trouble with brakes from the start. The Foyt/Bucknum automatic car was in for a change of pads and had the system bled a short while after the start, a procedure which had to be repeated on numerous occasions. With these delays the car finished twelfth, a total of 36 laps behind the winner.

Sutcliffe blew the engine of his privately entered GT 40 in the hairpin, and two laps later Stewart in the Alan Mann GT 40 spun on the oil and the back of the car burst into flame. The fire was quickly controlled and Stewart drove back to the pits to hand over to Graham Hill.

McLean in the Comstock GT 40 spun at the same spot and he too caught fire, this time with tragic results. By the time the fire was under control the driver was dead and the other Comstock car was withdrawn shortly afterward.

Gurney built up a lead of over 2 minutes and the P3 Ferrari could make no impression on the Ford. These two cars were the only ones on the same lap. In third place was the MK II roadster driven by Miles and Ruby.

The Ferrari began to have gearbox trouble and shortly after was out of the race. The order then became Gurney/Grant in first, Miles/Ruby in second, Hansgen/Donohue, third, with fourth place being held by the Revson/Scott GT 40, which led the Sports class.

Six minutes from the end of the race the drive chain to the scavenge pump in the leading Ford broke and the pan filled with oil. The car came to a halt on the circuit, not far from the timekeeper at the hairpin, and Gurney broke a standing regulation by pushing the car back to the pits. Miles covered two laps in the last six minutes, putting him one lap ahead of Gurney. The first provisional results showed Miles first ahead of Gurney. However, the stewards met and the car which had led most of the race was disqualified. Ken Miles and Lloyd Ruby won the race at the new record speed of 98.631 mph, and Gurney was credited with the fastest lap 2 min. 54 sec. (107.09 mph). Hansgen/Donohue were second and the Revson/Scott GT 40 third, an all together satisfactory result for the Ford team.

Some of the vast quantity of equipment needed for a full team effort at Le Mans. (Ford Motor Co.)

There were more than 30,000 spectators at the Le Mans test weekend on April 2–3, 1966. The Ford contingent for this practice session was made up of two modified GT 40's with 4.7-liter engines from the Alan Mann stable, two 7-liter MK II cars entered by Shelby-American, and numerous privately entered GT 40's. However, star of the show was the new car which was handled directly by Dearborn. This was the long-awaited J-car which had little in common with the GT 40.

The Alan Mann team's 4.7-liter Fords were modified with aluminum side panels in place of the fiberglass units, and numerous small weight-saving efforts that made them 120 pounds lighter than the production cars. They were finished in red with gold stripes and were, as raced at Sebring, still carrying the quick-action oil pipe connectors protruding from the offside of the body through which oil could be squirted straight into the sump during a pit stop.

The two Shelby-American cars were the 7-liter MK II's already seen at Sebring and Daytona; both cars used Ford's own 4-speed gearbox. One of these cars was completely destroyed when Walt Hansgen crashed down the escape road beyond the pits; he suffered multiple injuries from which he later died.

The Gurney/Grant MK II at the pits before the race, Le Mans, 1966. (Ford Motor Co.)

The Ford lineup, Le Mans, 1966. (Ford Motor Co.)

Drivers present for the Ford team were McLaren, Amon, Miles, and Lucien Bianchi. The Alan Mann team had on hand Graham Hill, Jackie Stewart, John Whitmore, Frank Gardner, and Paul Hawkins. The privately owned cars of Ford France were driven by Henri Greder and Guy Ligier and the Scuderia Filippinetti car by Willy Mairesse and Hermann Muller.

As there was no official Ferrari opposition at these tests and the Chaparral team was also missing, the Fords had things their own way, the only disappointment being the J-car, which showed that it was not ready for competition and consequently was not entered for the actual Le Mans race.

The 1966 Le Mans 24 Hour race was held on June 18–19 and Ford came prepared to do battle with Ferrari in a much more organized manner than in the previous years.

There were eight of the 7-liter (427 cu. in.) MK II coupes, the Ford team being split into three, with Shelby-American entering three cars, Holman & Moody another three, plus two more from Alan Mann Racing of England. All the cars were built to the same specification, differing only in color for identification purposes.

The Shelby-American drivers were Ken Miles/Denis Hulme in a light-blue car, Bruce McLaren/Chris Amon in a black car, and Dan Gurney/Jerry Grant in a red car.

Holman & Moody drivers were Paul Hawkins/Mark Donohue in a bronze car, Ron Bucknum/Dick Hutcherson in a gold car, and Lucien Bianchi/Mario Andretti in a royal-blue car.

Graham Hill and Brian Muir drove the silver Alan Mann entry and John Whitmore and Frank Gardner the yellow car from the same stable. These eight MK II's were supported by five GT 40's in private hands.

Major opposition was from the factory and North American

Close-up of the Le Mans lineup, 1966. (Ford Motor Co.)

Just 10 minutes before 4 P.M. on race day at Le Mans, 1966. (Ford Motor Co.)

As the flag falls, a group of Fords are away first. (Ford Motor Co.)

Racing Team Ferraris, three of which were the latest P3 models, and four other privately entered P2 Ferraris.

Ford had some driver problems as A. J. Foyt, Lloyd Ruby, and Jackie Stewart had been scheduled for the team but injuries in previous races had sidelined them. During practice, Graham Hill's original codriver Dick Thompson was disqualified as he was involved in an accident and did not comply with the rules that required him to make a report. Brian Muir was picked as a replacement.

In practice, the Fords showed that they were going to be hard to beat if they stayed together. Dan Gurney turned a lap at 3 min. 30.6 sec., an average speed of 142.8 mph. The other Fords were close behind with the team Ferraris mixed in the group, managing only fifth, seventh, eighth, and fifteenth fastest times.

As the flag fell and the drivers sprinted to their cars, it was Graham Hill in the Alan Mann MK II that laid long black streaks of rubber as he accelerated into the lead.

Graham Hill came by leading the first lap with Gurney behind him, the two of them running away from the field. However, lap 1 held an unpleasant omen for Ford as three of the Dearborn cars came into the pits first time around. Ken Miles pulled in with the light-blue MK II to have the door shut properly, Whitmore brought his MK II in and stayed for a while to have a broken brake pipe repaired, and Hawkins brought in the bronze Holman & Moody car with a broken differential to retire.

After half an hour of racing the three Fords of Gurney, Hill, and Bucknum were already out of sight of the fourth-place Ferrari driven by Rodriguez. Miles was making up time fast after his pit stop, and laps of about 3 min. 33 sec. were being turned although Ford strategy had called for laps of 3 min. 36 sec. in the early stages.

Miles set a new race record with a lap at 3 min. 33.1 sec. and moved up into fifth place behind Rodriguez' Ferrari. A Chaparral followed in sixth, then the two works Ferraris of Mike Parkes and Jean Guichet and the MK II Fords of McLaren and Bianchi running at a more sedate pace.

The situation at 5 P.M. was Ford, Ford, Ford, Ferrari, Ford, Chaparral, Ferrari, Ferrari, Ford, and Ford.

During the second hour it began to rain and the Whitmore/ Gardner and Hawkins/Donohue Fords were both repaired and back in the race. Neither of them ran well and they headed for the pits just as the leaders were due to refuel. This caused a good deal of confusion in the pits, and when Graham Hill brought his MK II in to refuel there was no room left and he had to carry on for one more lap before he could pit.

Mario Andretti at the wheel of the MK II he shared with Lucien Bianchi.
They retired with engine trouble after 8 hours. (Ford Motor Co.)

After the pit stops the P3 Ferrari of Rodriguez/Ginther moved up to third place, with Ginther doing his best in the face of overwhelming numbers.

Denis Hulme took over from Ken Miles and took the lead from Gurney's partner, Jerry Grant.

Even before darkness fell the pace began to take its toll. Ford No. 4 of Hawkins/Donohue was out with a broken differential and the No. 8 car of Whitmore/Gardner was further delayed by a defective clutch-operating mechanism which put the car behind the minimum regulation distance.

Before midnight there were more retirements. Graham Hill walked back to the pits having left No. 7 out on the circuit with broken suspension and the Bianchi/Andretti No. 6 was out with a blown engine.

At midnight Gurney/Grant were back in the lead, Miles/Hulme were second, and the Ferrari third all on the same lap. The McLaren/Amon Ford was one lap behind with two more Ferraris following at four and five laps' distance, respectively.

By 1 A.M. the Rodriguez/Ginther Ferrari was out with gearbox trouble and one of the Essex Racing Team GT 40's was out with a blown engine. Another Ferrari went out with a broken brake pipe, and as dawn broke the Fords filled the first six places. Ford lost a steady runner when the Ligier/Grossman GT 40 went out with engine trouble, but at the same time the remaining P3 Ferrari, which was suffering from an internal water leak in the engine and a slipping clutch, finally succumbed at 8 A.M.

Another Ford went out with Spoerry crashing the Scuderia Filippinetti GT 40 which he had been sharing with Peter Sutcliffe.

There was consternation in the pits as the Gurney/Grant Ford began to show signs of failing and there was gloom in the Shelby pits as car No. 3 came in slowly to retire, having lost its water, overheated, and was unable to replenish due to the rule requiring a certain distance between taking on fluids other than gasoline. Fords were still in the first three places.

The Scott/Revson GT-40 retired with an oil leak. Le Mans, 1966. (Ford Motor Co.)

The McLaren/Amon MK II led the race at the 13th hour. Le Mans, 1966. (Ford Motor Co.)

The rains came in the afternoon slowing the pace. Le Mans, 1966.
(Ford Motor Co.)

At noon, with four hours still to go, there were only 16 cars left running, the three Fords, with the McLaren/Amon car now slightly ahead of the Miles/Hulme car; the Bucknum/Hutcherson car was nine laps behind and then came a raft of Porsches.

By 2 P.M. rain started to fall and everyone began to go very gently. However, the rain stopped in the final hour leaving the roads awash and the leading Fords threw up great rooster tails as they circulated at a reduced pace.

During the last half hour the two Shelby cars closed up together, Miles waiting for McLaren who had lost the lead during the final pit stops for refueling and the light-blue and the black 7-liter Ford circulated quietly together gathering up the gold car of Bucknum as they started what was going to be their last lap and a well-deserved victory for Ford.

The winning MK II drifts through the esses. Le Mans, 1966. (Ford Motor Co.)

The McLaren/Amon MK II ran a steady second until the last lap when it won by a matter of yards. Le Mans, 1966. (Ford Motor Co.)

The Miles/Hulme MK II running in the rain. The team moved into 1st place at 18 hours. Le Mans, 1966. (Ford Motor Co.)

By a prearranged plan, the Fords of McLaren and Miles arrived with headlights ablaze, in as near a dead heat as they could judge, with Bucknum just behind them. It was impressive and an undisputed victory.

The celebration was somewhat damped when the timekeepers announced that McLaren and Amon had won, a dead heat being impossible as the cars had started at 4 P.M. on Saturday with the Miles/Hulme car already some yards ahead of the starting grid so that as they arrived side by side on the same lap on Sunday at 4 P.M., the McLaren/Amor car must have covered a greater distance in the 24 hours, the difference being quoted as 20 meters. The staging by the Shelby team had backfired.

As Ford had won the 1966 Manufacturers Championship, Ferrari decided to offer a full challenge and send a team of his latest cars for the first major event of 1967, the Daytona Continental 24 Hour Race.

The McLaren/Amon MK II rejoins the race after a pit stop. Le Mans, 1966. (Ford Motor Co.)

Sequence showing the controversial finish of the 1966 Le Mans race as Ford tried for a dead heat. The sequence shows that the McLaren/ Amon car led the Miles/Hulme and Bucknum/Hutcherson cars across the line. (Ford Motor Co.)

Several days were set aside for practice, with Thursday as qualifying day. The Ford team consisted of six MK II Fords entered by Shelby American and Holman & Moody. Each car was painted a different color for quick identification. The drivers were McLaren/Bianchi, Bucknum/Gardner, Foyt/Gurney, Donohue/Revson, Andretti/Ginther, and Ruby/Hulme. Three private GT 40's were also entered, one being J. W. Engineering's GT 40 driven by Dick Thompson and Jackie Ickx.

The MK II's had undergone certain modifications at the expense of weight. In the cockpit there was a roll cage of heavy construction. An improved instrument panel was fitted and by the side of the driver was a large fixed gas extinguisher, designed to keep fire out of the cockpit long enough for a driver to be rescued in the event

Hulme waves to the crowd, not realizing that the timekeepers have declared the dead heat invalid and that he and Ken Miles had lost the race by about two yards. (Ford Motor Co.)

of an accident. The oil tank, formerly in the forward compartment, was moved to the rear and positioned at the left of the engine. Other than moving some of the weight to the back, this also got rid of a major heat source from the front.

The 7-liter Ford engines also produced more power and were fitted with two four-barrel carburetors. The extra power, which put the total over 500 bhp, was needed to push along the 200 plus more pounds of extra weight on the 1967 MK II's.

The Shelby cars had the high rear airscoops to the brakes removed, and to overcome the increased "G" loads on the banking, two ideas were used to stop the cars from bottoming. On the Shelby cars a lug on the center of the antiroll bar pressed on a stop when the car was well down on the springs, which had the effect of stiffen-

The Bucknum/Hutcherson MK II finished in 3d place, making it a 1-2-3-victory for Ford. Le Mans, 1966. (Ford Motor Co.)

ing the last inch of movement. Holman & Moody had a similar idea
but they had an extra connection on the right rear wheel and a short
torsion bar to the center stop. This had the effect of leaving the
antiroll bar to function normally while the torsion bar came into use
only when the right suspension was almost on the stop. One car
from each team had "Mercury" on the side stripes instead of
"Ford." Practice started on Tuesday with qualifying on Thursday.

It became obvious that the Ferraris were lapping consistently
faster than the Fords and this caused concern in the Ford pits. With
two Ferraris and Jim Hall's Chaparral faster than the best Ford,
Gurney's car was set up as a sprint car. The tires were changed for
some Goodyear short-life "sticky" ones and the fuel was cut to a
minimum for a few laps. Gurney succeeded in getting pole position

Pit practice, Daytona, 1967. (Ford Motor Co.)

by 0.26 second but his engine had to be changed afterward. Gurney's time was 1 min. 55.10 sec., an average speed of 119.165 mph. The next Ford was Andretti's in fifth place on the grid at 117.889 mph, followed in seventh place by McLaren at 117.530 mph, Bucknum in ninth with 116.724 mph, and Ruby in tenth with 116.632 mph.

On Saturday, February 4, 1967, the 3 P.M. start approached and the cars lined up on a dummy grid in the pits, and just before three o'clock they made off to do one complete lap and then start on the green flag on the backstretch.

As the green flag fell, the Ford of Foyt and Phil Hill's Chaparral shot forward onto the banking; before they had completed the first lap the Chaparral had a lead of 50 yards.

Andretti had been given the job of going into the lead and breaking up the opposition, but however much as he tried he could not keep his Ford up with the Chaparral, which continued to pull away at the rate of a second every two laps.

When the first pit stop was made Spence took over from Phil Hill and was still in the lead when he left the pits.

Andretti headed for the pit after 30 minutes of racing as his car began to handle badly. A front-tire change did nothing to improve the situation and a few laps later he was back in the pits for a rear-wheel change. This immediately improved the handling, as the left rear tire had a cut in it which was causing it to deflate.

On lap 15 Bucknum came into the pits complaining of transmission trouble, and eight laps later he was back and had no third or fourth gears.

The output shaft had sheared and the mechanics set about replacing the whole gearbox. As the leaders completed lap 42, Bucknum was in the race again but right at the end of the field.

McLaren's Ford was overheating when he made his first pit

stop. From then onward water was added at every stop and in the last hours stops were made every 20 laps. A cylinder head gasket had blown in the early stages, and it was thought to be only a matter of time before the sick car was retired; as it happened, it was the only factory Ford to finish.

Donohue ran into suspension trouble on lap 62 and was in for a long time as a shock absorber was replaced. Then the Andretti-Ginther car came into the pits with no third or fourth gears and the gearbox was replaced. A short while afterward Ruby made an unscheduled stop and his gearbox was changed. In each case the output shaft had sheared in exactly the same place. An outside contractor was responsible for the faulty finishing and heat treatment.

Before dawn every factory-entered Ford had its gearbox replaced. As the replacements broke the cars were withdrawn, for not even Ford had an unlimited supply of spare gearboxes.

At dawn the Foyt/Gurney car was lapping fourth and the Mc-Laren/Bianchi car in ninth. Just after 8 A.M. Foyt/Gurney were out when their engine blew up. This left only one of the original six cars, and it was taking on almost as much water as fuel, for the leak in the gasket was pouring away water extremely fast.

The three leading Ferraris crossed the line together to make it a clean sweep for the Italian company. The Thompson/Ickx GT 40 was sixth, 8 laps ahead of the seventh-place MK II of McLaren/Bianchi, with the Wonder/Caldwell GT 40 in eighth place, 21 laps behind the MK II. The general opinion was that the defeat would do some good, as there had been some members of the factory team that thought Ford was invincible.

With Ferrari having come out on top at Daytona with their 1-2-3 victory, it was unfortunate that none of the Italian factory cars participated at Sebring on April 1, 1967. The North American

Daytona, 1967, was a disaster for Ford. The best-placed MK II was 7th, driven by McLaren and Bianchi. (Ford Motor Co.)

The McLaren/Bianchi moves his MK II inside the Chaparral. Daytona, 1967. (Ford Motor Co.)

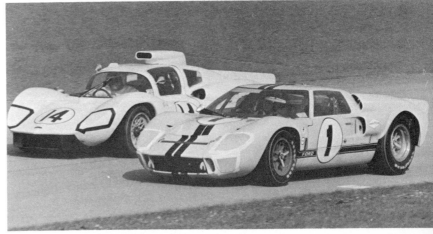

A short while later the Mc-Laren/Bianchi MK II has opened a wide gap on the Chaparral. (Ford Motor Co.)

Racing Team Ferraris also decided not to attend, as there was the problem of a lawsuit over an accident which happened the previous year. The only Ferrari opposition to Ford was David Piper with a P2 and four private Dinos running in the 2-liter class.

The real opposition came from the two Chaparrals, a 2F driven by Jim Hall and Mike Spence and a 2D driven by Johnson/Jennings. Ford entered the new MK IV development of the J-car

The MK IV, a development of the J-Car, won the 12-Hours of Sebring in 1967. It was the car's first racing appearance and was driven by Mario Andretti and Bruce McLaren. (Ford Motor Co.)

Umberto Maglioli, Ford GT-40. Sebring, 1967. (Ford Motor Co.)

with honeycomb-sandwich construction but with manual transmission. This car was driven by Andretti and McLaren, while Foyt
and Ruby drove a backup Ford MK II; both had the 7-liter (427
cu. in.) engine.

GT 40's were entered by Maglioli/Vaccarella, Grossman/Mc-
Namara, Wonder/Caldwell, and Thompson/Lowther. Both Andretti and McLaren unofficially broke the lap record in the MK IV
when they set identical times of 2 min. 48 sec., an average speed
of 111.42 mph and some 6.8 seconds better than Gurney's record
with the MK II Ford in 1966.

The 2d place in the 1967 Sebring 12-Hour race went to the Ford MK II of Foyt and Ruby. (Ford Motor Co.)

A. J. Foyt, Ford MK II. Sebring, 1967. (Ford Motor Co.)

A slower competitor is sandwiched between the Foyt/Ruby Ford MK II and a Ferrari. Sebring, 1967. (Ford Motor Co.)

The Foyt/Ruby MK II and the two Chaparrals were also below the previous record.

After the parades were over the 12-hour classic got underway. The 2-liter Alfa Romeo shot into the lead and maintained it for two laps when Foyt in the MK II Ford took over with Alfa second, Thompson's Ford GT 40 third, and Piper's Ferrari fourth. The Chaparral 2F had starting trouble on the line and lost over half a minute. The Texan car made up ground fast and by one hour was fourth behind Andretti, who had a 30-second lead over the MK II Ford and the Piper Ferrari.

By quarter distance the Chaparral was in the lead with the Texan car and the MK IV Ford on the same lap. McLaren had set the lap record at 109.05 mph.

On lap 65 the Piper Ferrari gave out and the Chaparral fell to third when it stopped for Hall to take over. The big battle now began and in the next two hours the lap record was shattered 20 times. The two Fords made pit stops for fuel and the Chaparral was back in the lead, but after the stop McLaren put pressure on Hall and closed the gap so that when Hall had to stop for fuel the two Fords were back out front.

Spence matched the furious pace when he took over from Hall and set a new lap record at 111.032 mph but the automatic transmission oil began to boil. As the Chaparral 2F retired so did the companion 2D and the Fords were able to ease off.

When darkness fell around 8 P.M. the Andretti/McLaren Ford led the Foyt/Ruby MK II by three laps.

At 11:30 P.M. there was drama in the pits when the MK II came in with expensive noises from the engine—a camshaft had broken. At midnight the Andretti/McLaren car took the checkered flag with a Porsche 12 laps behind in what was generally accepted as second place. Eventually the timekeepers announced that the Foyt/Ruby MK II had in fact retained its second place as it had covered the same amount of laps 266, but was 8 seconds ahead on total time.

The Maglioli/Vaccarella GT 40 finished fifth and first in the Sports class. Grossman/McNamara finished eighth and the GT's of Wonder/Caldwell and Thompson/Lowther retired their car with engine problems.

On April 8–9, 1967, the Automobile Club de l'Quest held the Le Mans test weekend and some 30,000 spectators again turned out to see the action.

The GT-40 of Maglioli and Vaccarella finished 5th and won its class. Sebring, 1967. (Ford Motor Co.)

Grossman and McNamara finished 8th with their GT-40. Sebring, 1967. (Ford Motor Co.)

The Wonder/Caldwell GT-40 retired with engine trouble. Sebring, 1967. (Ford Motor Co.)

With Ford's victory at Sebring and Ferrari's win at Daytona, the score was even and the stage was being set for an all-out battle at Le Mans and both teams were there in force for practice. Ford brought two cars a MK IV and a MK II, the former looked after by Shelby-American and the latter by Holman & Moody. The MK IV was identical to the winning car at Sebring, even to being painted bright yellow. It was driven by McLaren and was fully instrumented on practically all the moving parts and wired to a Chrondek recorder which taped all information for analysis by a mobile laboratory behind the pits.

Signposts and hay bales show that Le Mans is a true road circuit.
(Ford Motor Co.)

The MK II was driven by Mark Donohue and was similar to the 1966 winner. It was painted gold and already looked a little out of date. Added to the two factory Fords were the highly modified Mirage-Fords entered by J. W. Automotive Engineering of England. These were basically GT 40's reworked by John Wyer with a lighter chassis and scheduled to be fitted with 5-liter engines for the race. For practice they used normal 4.7-liter engines; drivers were Dick Attwood and David Piper.

The Saturday practice session was held under perfect conditions and the Ferraris quickly reduced the 1966 lap record of 3 min. 30.6 sec. to 3 min. 25.5 sec., an average speed of 146.5 mph.

The Sebring-winning MK IV at the Le Mans test day, 1967. (Ford Motor Co.)

The Fords made no attempt to do any really fast laps. However, McLaren's MK IV was timed on the Mulsanne Straight at 205 mph compared to the fastest Ferrari time of 198 mph. McLaren was confident of beating the Ferrari lap speed whenever he wanted to, knowing how much he had in reserve and estimated that he could pull 215 mph down the straight and was confident of getting a lap speed of about 3 min. 22 sec.

Unfortunately, Sunday dawned wet and cold and it stayed that way throughout the day. McLaren did only a few slow exploratory laps.

The lineup of MK IV Fords at Le Mans, 1967. (Ford Motor Co.)

On paper, Ferrari left Le Mans on top, but no one was fooled by the freak circumstances and Ford had every reason to be optimistic for the big race.

The excellent performance of the MK IV at Sebring allowed Ford some optimism for the outcome of the big battle with Ferrari at Le Mans on June 10–11, 1967. Ford hoped to repeat the previous year's 1-2-3 finish, but Ferrari had shown that his new P4 models, although smaller in engine capacity, were nevertheless formidable rivals. The Phil Hill/Spence Chaparral promised to enliven matters and the Lola-Aston Martin driven by John Surtees was a very fast dark horse.

The MK IV Ford entry was made up of Gurney/Foyt, McLaren/Donohue, Andretti/Bianchi, Gardner/McCluskey, and Ruby/Hulme. Hawkins/Bucknum and Schlesser/Ligier drove revised MK IIB's, the major modification being the installation of the MK IV's type 530-bhp engine. Two Mirage-Fords with 5.7-liter engines were entered for Piper/Thompson and Ickx/Muir, while Greder/Dumay, Maglioli/Casoni, and Salmon/Redman had GT 40's. To counter this, Ferrari entered three of his P4's and a P3/4 was allocated to the Equipe Nationale Belge.

The Ford team experienced a great deal of windshield problems during practice but this was corrected by a new batch of properly tempered screens being flown in from the U.S.A.

McLaren then took out one of the MK IV's and lapped in 3 min. 24.4 sec., an average of 147.316 mph, during which time the car was timed at 215 mph on the Mulsanne Straight. This was faster than Bandini's record time of 3 min. 25.5 sec. during the Le Mans test session in April.

All the cars performed well and the starting lineup saw Ford holding five of the first six. It was warm but overcast for the start at 4 P.M. on June 10.

As the drivers made their sprint to the lined-up cars it was the Rodriguez Ferrari that was off first, but before he had gone far Paul Hawkins was ahead with the MK IIB.

As they came around the first time it was Hawkins ahead of Gardner's Ford, Rodriguez, Schlesser in the other MK IIB, and Gurney in the MK IV.

After an hour's racing the Hawkins/Bucknum Ford still led with the Gurney/Foyt car in second place, the McLaren/Donohue MK IV third, and the Hill/Spence Chaparral had moved up to fourth. The Amon/Vaccarella and Rodriguez/Baghetti P4 Ferraris were fifth and sixth.

The Fords stopped for fuel and the Chaparral was in first place. A rapid check revealed that the Fords had tankage for about one hour's running while the Chaparral and the Ferraris could run about 15 minutes longer. After the second refueling session the Gurney/Foyt Ford led and the Andretti/Bianchi MK IV moved ahead of the Chaparral into second. Both Lola-Aston Martins retired and both Mirage-Fords retired with engine trouble, the Salmon/Redman GT 40 was out after crashing and catching fire. The three Fords and the Chaparral made it an all-American lead group, but the Ferraris were playing a waiting game, two of them being on the same lap as the fourth-place Chaparral.

Shortly before the start. Le Mans, 1967. (Ford Motor Co.)

The Hawkins/Bucknum MK II led the first hour, retired with oil shortage. Le Mans, 1967. (Ford Motor Co.)

The Andretti/Bianchi MK IV held 2d place at one time, started a multiple crash that eliminated three Fords. (Ford Motor Co.)

The Piper/Thompson Mirage-Ford retired with engine trouble after 4 hours. (Ford Motor Co.)

At 11 P.M., after refueling stops, the Parkes/Scarfiotti Ferrari took over the lead, but by 1 A.M. the three Fords were back in first, second, and third places.

At 2 A.M. it was still 1-2-3 for Ford, with the leaders' lap times running around 3 min. 30 sec. The pattern seemed set when Bianchi brought the No. 3 Ford in for fuel and new brake pads. Andretti took over and on braking for the esses one brake grabbed and he bounced off one bank into the other, completely wrecking the car. Next man on the scene was McCluskey in Ford No. 5, who spun and hit Andretti's wreckage. Immediately after this Schlesser came around with the MK IIB and ran that into the wreckage, three Fords out in one lap. Of the three drivers, only Andretti was slightly injured.

At half distance the scene had thus changed completely. The Gurney/Foyt Ford was well in the lead, but three Ferraris and a Chaparral now filled the space between the first-place car and the next Ford in sixth place.

As dawn came it was still Gurney/Foyt, then the Parkes/ Scarfiotti Ferrari, the Hill/Spence Chaparral followed by another Ferrari, then a Ford and another Ferrari.

At 5:30 A.M. the Chaparral's role as a serious competitor ended when it came to a halt in the pits for three hours to have a new seal fitted on the gearbox. After rejoining the race it finally retired with most of the transmission oil gone.

At 6:30 A.M. the Gurney/Foyt Ford was leading the second-place Ferrari by seven laps and comfortably averaging 137 mph, but Ferraris held second, third, and fourth. With six hours to go, the second-place Ferrari had made up some ground and was only five laps behind.

There was a moment of panic in the pits when the McLaren/

Donohue Ford lost its rear body panels and the whole thing had to be taped back together. When the Sutcliffe/Klass Ferrari broke its gearbox, the McLaren/Donohue Ford was back in fourth place. Gurney made a quick pit stop for fuel and to hand over to Foyt. At this period the Ferrari was lapping at 10 seconds a lap faster than the leading Ford, but with the leading cars stopping for fuel for the last time and 90 minutes left to go, the Ferrari slowed its pace to that of the Ford as there were still some 34 miles to catch up to the American entry.

The Gurney/Foyt MK IV led the race from the 2d hour to the finish. Le Mans, 1967. (Ford Motor Co.)

The view that the opposition had of the Gurney/Foyt MK IV. Le Mans, 1967. (Ford Motor Co.)

Dan Gurney, A. J. Foyt, and a Ford MK IV made an all-American victory at record speed. (Ford Motor Co.)

As the Gurney/Foyt Ford MK IV was given the flag at the end of 24 hours, it marked first all-American win ever in the classic race. Gurney and Foyt had obliterated the record by a 10-mph margin, winning at an average speed of 135.483 mph and covering a record distance of 3,251.563 miles.

It was worth it! Mrs. Ford, Giovanni Agnelli of Fiat, and Henry Ford II after the Le Mans victory, 1967. (Ford Motor Co.)

Results of Four-Cylinder Fords, 1922 — 36 Indianapolis 500

	Position	Driver	Automobile	Laps	Qualifying Speed
1922	14	Jack Curtner	FRONTY-FORD	160	D.N.Q.
	18	C. Glenn Howard	FRONTY-FORD	165	83.900
1923	5	L. L. Corum	BARBER-WARNOCK-FORD	200	86.650
1924	14	Bill Hunt	BARBER-WARNOCK-FORD	191	85.040
	16	Alfred Moss	BARBER-WARNOCK-FORD	177	85.270
	17	Fred Harder	BARBER-WARNOCK-FORD	177	82.770
1925	21	M. C. Jones	SKELLY-FORD	33	88.478
1926	25	Jack McCarver	HAMLIN-FORD	23	86.418
1930	13	Chet Miller	FRONTY-FORD	161	97.360
1931	23	Gene Haustein	FRONTY-FORD	117	108.395
1936	26	Frank McGurk	ABELS AUTO FORD	51	113.102

Results of V-8 Fords, 1934 — 47 Indianapolis 500

	Position	Driver	Automobile	Laps	Qualifying Speed
1934	16	Charles Crawford	DETROIT GASKET-FORD	110	108.784
	33	Chet Miller	BOHNALITE-FORD	33	109.252
1935	16	Ted Horn	MILLER-FORD	145	133.213
	24	Johnny Seymour	MILLER-FORD	71	112.696
	26	George Bailey	MILLER-FORD	65	113.432
	29	Bob Sall	MILLER-FORD	47	110.519
1946	21	Danny Kladis	GRANCOR-V8	46	118.890
1947	12	Pete Romcevich	CAMCO MOTORS-FORD	168	117.218

Results of Indianapolis 500, 1963 — 67

	Position	Driver	Laps	Time	Average
1963	2	Jim Clark	200	3:30:09.24	142.752
	7	Dan Gurney	200	3:34:10.81	140.071
1964	2	Rodger Ward	200	3:25:00.18	146.339
	17	Dan Gurney	110		
	24	Jim Clark	47		
	25	Bobby Marshman	39		
	26	Eddie Johnson	6		
	29	Dave MacDonald	1		
	30	Eddie Sachs	1		
1965	1	Jim Clark	200	3:19:05.34	150.686
	2	Parnelli Jones	200	3:21:04.32	149.200
	3	Mario Andretti	200	3:21:10.70	149.121
	4	Al Miller	200	3:24:39.89	146.581
	7	Bobby Johns	197		
	8	Don Branson	197		
	9	Al Unser	196		
	11	Lloyd Ruby	184		
	12	Len Sutton	177		
	13	Johnny Boyd	140		
	15	A. J. Foyt	115		
	16	Bud Tinglestad	115		

	Position	Driver	Laps	Time	Average
	23	Masten Gregory	59		
	26	Dan Gurney	42		
	29	Joe Leonard	27		
	30	Roger McCluskey	18		
	31	Johnny Rutherford	15		
1966	1	Graham Hill	200	3:27:52.33	144.317
	2	Jim Clark	200	3:28:33.66	143.843
	3	Jim McElreath	200	3:28:42.42	143.742
	4	Gordon Johncock	200	3:29:40.00	143.456
	6	Jackie Stewart	190		
	9	Joe Leonard	170		
	10	Jerry Grant	167		
	11	Lloyd Ruby	166		
	12	Al Unser	161		
	13	Roger McCluskey	129		
	16	Carl Williams	38		
	18	Mario Andretti	27		
	19	George Snider	22		
	20	Chuck Hulse	22		
	22	Johnny Boyd	5		
	—	Don Branson	0		
	—	Billy Foster	0		
	—	Gary Corgdon	0		
	—	A. J. Foyt	0		
	—	Dan Gurney	0		
	—	Arnie Knepper	0		

Position		Driver	Laps	Time	Average
	—	Al Miller	0		
	—	Cale Yarborough	0		
	—	Larry Dickson	0		
	—	Ronnie Duman	0		
1967	1	A. J. Foyt	200	3:18:24.22	151.207
	2	Al Unser	198	3:18:10.55	149.867
	3	Joe Leonard	197	3:18:02.07	149.216
	4	Denis Hulme	197	3:18:11.07	149.102
	5	Jim McElreath	197	3:18:30.63	148.859
	9	Bobby Unser	193		
	10	Carl Williams	189		
	15	Larry Dickson	180		
	17	Cale Yarborough	176		
	18	Jackie Stewart	168		
	19	Roger McCluskey	165		
	20	Jerry Grant	162		
	21	Dan Gurney	158		
	24	Jochen Rindt	108		
	25	Johnny Rutherford	103		
	26	George Snider	99		
	27	Lee Roy Yarbrough	87		
	28	Al Miller	74		
	30	Mario Andretti	58		
	31	Jim Clark	35		
	32	Graham Hill	3		

Qualification Times at Indianapolis 500, 1963 — 67

	Driver	Automobile	Mph
1963	Jim Clark	LOTUS-FORD	149.750
	Dan Gurney	LOTUS-FORD	149.019
1964	Jim Clark	LOTUS-FORD	158.828
	Bobby Marshman	LOTUS-FORD	157.867
	Rodger Ward	WATSON-FORD	156.406
	Dan Gurney	LOTUS-FORD	154.487
	Dave MacDonald	THOMPSON-FORD	151.464
	Eddie Sachs	HALIBRAND-FORD	151.439
	Eddie Johnson	THOMPSON-FORD	152.905
1965	A. J. Foyt	LOTUS-FORD	161.233
	Jim Clark	LOTUS-FORD	160.729
	Dan Gurney	LOTUS-FORD	158.898
	Mario Andretti	BRAWNER-FORD	158.849
	Parnelli Jones	LOTUS-FORD	158.625
	Al Miller	LOTUS-FORD	157.805
	Lloyd Ruby	HALIBRAND-FORD	157.246
	Johnny Rutherford	HALIBRAND-FORD	156.291
	Len Sutton	VOLLSTEDT-FORD	156.121
	Don Branson	WATSON-FORD	155.501
	Bobby Johns	LOTUS-FORD	155.481

Driver	Automobile	Mph
Roger McCluskey	HALIBRAND-FORD	155.186
Bud Tinglestad	LOLA-FORD	154.672
Joe Leonard	HALIBRAND-FORD	154.268
Johnny Boyd	BRP-FORD	155.172
Masten Gregory	BRP-FORD	154.540
Al Unser	LOLA-FORD	154.440

	Driver	Automobile	Mph
1966	Mario Andretti	BRAWNER-FORD	165.899
	Jim Clark	LOTUS-FORD	164.144
	George Snider	LOTUS-FORD	162.521
	Lloyd Ruby	EAGLE-FORD	162.455
	Gordon Johncock	GERHARDT-FORD	161.059
	Jim McElreath	BRABHAM-FORD	160.908
	Chuck Hulse	WATSON-FORD	160.844
	Don Branson	GERHARDT-FORD	160.385
	Jerry Grant	EAGLE-FORD	160.335
	Jackie Stewart	LOLA-FORD	159.972
	Billy Foster	VOLLSTEDT-FORD	159.490
	Johnny Boyd	BRP-FORD	159.384
	Graham Hill	LOLA-FORD	159.243
	A. J. Foyt	LOTUS-FORD	161.355
	Dan Gurney	EAGLE-FORD	160.499
	Joe Leonard	EAGLE-FORD	159.560
	Roger McCluskey	EAGLE-FORD	159.271
	Al Unser	LOTUS-FORD	162.272
	Cale Yarborough	VOLLSTEDT-FORD	159.794

	Driver	Automobile	Mph
	Carl Williams	GERHARDT-FORD	159.645
	Arnie Knepper	CECIL-FORD	159.440
	Al Miller	LOTUS-FORD	158.681
	Larry Dickson	HALIBRAND-FORD	159.144
	Ronnie Duman	EISERT-FORD	158.646
1967	Mario Andretti	BRAWNER-FORD	168.982
	Dan Gurney	EAGLE-FORD	167.224
	Gordon Johncock	GERHARDT-FORD	166.559
	A. J. Foyt	COYOTE-FORD	166.289
	Joe Leonard	COYOTE-FORD	166.098
	Bobby Unser	EAGLE-FORD	164.752
	Al Unser	LOLA-FORD	164.594
	George Snider	MONGOOSE-FORD	164.256
	Jim McElreath	MOORE-FORD	164.256
	Jim Clark	LOTUS-FORD	163.213
	Arnie Knepper	CECIL-FORD	162.900
	Johnny Rutherford	EAGLE-FORD	162.859
	Cale Yarborough	VOLLSTEDT-FORD	162.830
	Larry Dickson	LOTUS-FORD	162.543
	Roger McCluskey	EAGLE-FORD	165.563
	Carl Williams	BRP-FORD	163.696
	Denis Hulme	EAGLE-FORD	163.376
	Bud Tinglestad	GERHARDT-FORD	163.228
	Lee Roy Yarbrough	VOLLSTEDT-FORD	163.066
	Jackie Stewart	LOLA-FORD	164.099

Driver	Automobile	Mph
Jerry Grant	EAGLE-FORD	163.808
Graham Hill	LOTUS-FORD	163.317
Jochen Rindt	EAGLE-GURNEY WESLAKE/FORD	163.051
Al Miller	GERHARDT-FORD	162.602

The Racing Record of the GT's and Prototypes

1964

May 31, Nürburgring 1,000 Km, Germany

P. Hill/McLaren	—	GT 40	retired

June 20–21, Le Mans 24 Hours, France

P. Hill/McLaren	—	GT 40	retired
Ginther/Gregory	—	GT 40	retired
Attwood/Schlesser	—	GT 40	retired

July 4–5, Reims 12 Hours, France

P. Hill/McLaren	—	GT 40	retired
Ginther/Gregory	—	GT 40	retired
Attwood/Schlesser	—	GT 40	retired

November 29, Nassau Tourist Trophy, Bahamas

P. Hill	—	GT 40	retired

1965

March 7, Daytona Continental 2,000 Km, U.S.A.

Miles/Ruby	1st	GT 40
Bondurant/Ginther	3d	GT 40

March 27, Sebring 12 Hours, U.S.A.

McLaren/Miles	2d	*GT 40*	
P. Hill/Ginther	—	*GT 40*	retired

April 25, Monza 1,000 Km, Italy

McLaren/Miles	3d	*GT 40*	
Amon/Maglioli	—	*GT 40*	retired

May 9, Targa Florio, Italy

Bondurant/Whitmore	—	*GT 40*	retired

May 23, Nürburgring 1,000 Km, Germany

Amon/Bucknum	8th	*GT 40*	
Trintignant/Ligier	—	*GT 40*	retired
P. Hill/McLaren	—	*GT 40*	retired
Attwood/Whitmore	—	*GT 40*	retired

June 6, Guards Trophy, Malloy Park, England

Attwood	2d	*GT 40*	

June 19–20, Le Mans 24 Hours, France

McLaren/Miles	—	*MK II*	retired
P. Hill/Amon	—	*MK II*	retired
Bondurant/Maglioli	—	*GT 40*	retired
Whitmore/Ireland	—	*GT 40*	retired
Trintignant/Ligier	—	*GT 40*	retired
Muller/Bucknum	—	*GT 40*	retired

August 25, Canadian Grand Prix, Mosport, Canada

Amon	—	*GT X1*	retired

October 31, Times Grand Prix, Riverside, U.S.A.

Amon	5th	*GT X1*
Scott	11th	*GT 40*

November 6, Kyalami 9 Hours, South Africa

Sutcliffe/Ireland	2d	*GT 40*

November 27, Nassau Speed Week, Bahamas

Amon	—	*GT X1*

December 6, Nassau Speed Week, Bahamas

Amon	—	*GT X1*

December 27, Pietermaritzburg 3 Hours, South Africa

Sutcliffe	—	*GT 40*

1966

February 5–6, Daytona Continental 24 Hours, U.S.A.

Miles/Ruby	1st	*MK II*	
Gurney/Grant	2d	*MK II*	
Hansgen/Donohue	3d	*MK II*	
McLaren/Amon	5th	*MK II*	
Bucknum/Ginther	—	*MK II*	retired
Sutcliffe/Grossman	9th	*GT 40*	
Revson/Gregory/Lowther	17th	*GT 40*	
Scott/Thompson	—		retired

March 26, Sebring 12 Hours, U.S.A.

Miles/Ruby	1st	*MK II*	
Hansgen/Donohue	2d	*MK II*	
Revson/Scott	3d	*GT 40*	
Grossman/Lowther	10th	*GT 40*	
Foyt/Bucknum	12th	*MK II*	
Holquist/Jennings/Kovaleski	13th	*GT 40*	
Payne/Cuomo	15th	*GT 40*	
Bentley/Byrne	22d	*GT 40*	
Gurney/Grant	—	*MK II*	retired
G. Hill/Stewart	—	*GT 40*	retired
Whitmore/Gardner	—	*GT 40*	retired
Pabst/Gregory	—	*GT 40*	retired
McLean/Oulette	—	*GT 40*	retired
Sutcliffe/Ireland	—	*GT 40*	retired
Wonder/Caldwell	—	*GT 40*	retired

April 8, Snetterton, Memorial Trophy, England

Attwood	3d	*GT 40*	

April 25, Monza 1,000 Km, Italy

Whitmore/Gregory	2d	*GT 40*	
Muller/Mairesse	3d	*GT 40*	
Ligier/Greder	6th	*GT 40*	
Scott/Revson	—	*GT 40*	retired
Ireland/Amon	—	*GT 40*	retired

April 30, Tourist Trophy, England

Sutcliffe	3d	*GT 40*	

May 7, Brands Hatch 500, England

Sutcliffe/Liddell	2d	*GT 40*	
Ireland/Amon	—	*GT 40*	retired

May 8, Targa Florio, Italy

Ligier/Greder	—	*GT 40*	retired

May 14, Silverstone, England

Scott	6th	*GT 40*	
Sutcliffe	—	*GT 40*	retired
Liddell	—	*GT 40*	retired

May 22, 1,000 Km of Spa, Belgium

Whitmore/Gardner	2d	*MK II*	
Scott/Revson	3d	*GT 40*	
Sutcliffe/Redman	4th	*GT 40*	
Ireland/Amon	5th	*GT 40*	
Mairesse/Muller	—	*GT 40*	retired
Hobbs/Neerpasch	—	*GT 40*	retired

May 28, Mallory Park, England

Sutcliffe	2d	*GT 40*	
Liddell	4th	*GT 40*	

June 5, Nürburgring 1,000 Km, Germany

Ligier/Schlesser	5th	*GT 40*	
Sutcliffe/J. Taylor	6th	*GT 40*	
Bond/Spence	12th	*GT 40*	
Whitmore/Neerpasch	—	*GT 40*	retired
Scott/Revson	—	*GT 40*	retired
Ireland/Salmon	—	*GT 40*	retired

June 18–19, Le Mans 24 Hours, France

McLaren/Amon	1st	MK II	
Miles/Hulme	2d	MK II	
Bucknum/Hutcherson	3d	MK II	
Hawkins/Donohue	—	MK II	retired
Whitmore/Gardner	—	MK II	retired
Bianchi/Andretti	—	MK II	retired
Gurney/Grant	—	MK II	retired
G. Hill/Muir	—	MK II	retired
Irelandt/Rindt	—	GT 40	retired
Ickx/Neerpasch	—	GT 40	retired
Ligier/Grossman	—	GT 40	retired
Scott/Revson	—	GT 40	retired
Sutcliffe/Shoerup	—	GT 40	retired

July 2, Crystal Palace, England

Sutcliffe	1st	GT 40
Liddell	2d	GT 40
Redman	3d	GT 40

July 9, Martini Trophy, Silverstone, England

Sutcliffe	6th	GT 40	
Liddell	7th	GT 40	
Bond	8th	GT 40	
Salmon	—	GT 40	retired

August 15, Wills Trophy, Croft, England

Liddell	1st	GT 40
Cussons	3d	GT 40

August 21, Surfer's Paradise 12 Hours, Australia

Sutcliffe/Matich	2d	GT 40

August 29, Eagle Trophy, Brands Hatch, England

Salmon	2d	GT 40
Ireland	4th	GT 40
Liddell	5th	GT 40

September 11, Austrian Grand Prix, Zeltweg, Austria

Salmon	4th	GT 40
Casoni	7th	GT 40
Rindt	9th	GT 40
Ireland	10th	GT 40

September 11, Zolder, Belgium

"Beurlys"	1st	GT 40

September 25, Coupe de Paris, Montlhery, France

Ireland	1st	GT 40

October 8, Dixon Trophy, Silverstone, England

Fry	2d	GT 40

October 16, 1,000 Km of Paris, Montlhery, France

Attwood/Schlesser	—	GT 40	retired
"Beurlys"/Mairesse	—	GT 40	retired
Vaccarella/Casoni	—	GT 40	retired

In 1966 Ford won the following championships: 1st. International Prototype Trophy, 1st. International Sports Car Championship

November 5, Kyalami 9 Hours, South Africa

Sutcliffe-Love	—	*GT 40*	retired
Nelson/Crabbe	—	*GT 40*	retired
Hobbs/Spence	—	*GT 40*	retired

November 26, Cape International 3 Hours, South Africa

Hobbs/Hailwood	—	*GT 40*	retired
Nelson/Crabbe	—	*GT 40*	retired

December 27, Pietermaritzburg 3 Hours, South Africa

Hailwood/Hobbs	1st	*GT 40*
Nelson/Crabbe	7th	*GT 40*

1967

February 4–5, Daytona Continental 24 Hours, U.S.A.

Thompson/Ickx	6th	*GT 40*	
McLaren/Bianchi/Gurney	7th	*MK II*	
Wonder/Caldwell	8th	*GT 40*	
Foyt/Gurney	—	*MK II*	retired
Andretti/Ginther	—	*MK II*	retired
Ruby/Hulme	—	*MK II*	retired
Casoni/Maglioli	—	*GT 40*	retired

March 23, Autosport Trophy, Snetterton, England

Hawkins	1st	*GT 40*
Hulme	2d	*GT 40*
Salmon	3d	*GT 40*
Harris	5th	*GT 40*
Nelson	6th	*GT 40*

March 27, Autosport Trophy, Silverstone, England

Hulme	1st	*GT 40*
Hawkins	2d	*GT 40*
Salmon	5th	*GT 40*
Harris	6th	*GT 40*

April 1, Sebring 12 Hours, U.S.A.

Andretti/McLaren	1st	*MK IV*	
Foyt/Ruby	2d	*MK II*	
Maglioli/Vaccarella	5th	*GT 40*	
Grossman/McNamara	8th	*GT 40*	
Thompson/Lowther	—	*GT 40*	retired
Wonder/Caldwell	—	*GT 40*	retired

April 8, GT Race, Snetterton, England

Crabbe	1st	*GT 40*

April 15, GT Race, Silverstone, England

Fry	1st	*GT 40*

April 25, 1,000 Km of Monza, Italy

Schlesser/Ligier	6th	*GT 40*	
Piper/Thompson	9th	*MIRAGE*	
Nelson/Liddell	11th	*GT 40*	
Ickx/Rees	—	*MIRAGE*	retired
Greder/Giorgi	—	*GT 40*	retired
Borel/Ballot-Lena	—	*GT 40*	retired
Drury/Oliver	—	*GT 40*	retired

May 1, 1,000 Km of Spa, Belgium

Ickx/Thompson	1st	*MIRAGE*	
Sutcliffe-Redman	6th	*GT 40*	
Salmon/Oliver	8th	*GT 40*	
Piper/Thompson	—	*MIRAGE*	retired
Schlesser/Ligier	—	*GT 40*	

May 14, Targa Florio, Italy

Greder/Giorgi	5th	*GT 40*

May 20, Martini Trophy, Silverstone, England

Hawkins	1st	*GT 40*	
Salmon	2d	*GT 40*	
Liddell	4th	*GT 40*	
Sutcliffe	7th	*GT 40*	
Gardner	—	*GT 40*	retired

May 28, Nürburgring 1,000 Km, Germany

Greder/Giorgi	7th	*GT 40*	
Crabbe/Pierpoint	8th	*GT 40*	
Schlesser/Ligier	10th	*GT 40*	
Nelson/DeKlerk	—	*GT 40*	retired

May 29, Group 4 Race, Crystal Palace, England

Hawkins	1st	*GT 40*	
Gardner	4th	*GT 40*	
Liddell	5th	*GT 40*	
Harris	8th	*GT 40*	
Sutcliffe	—	*GT 40*	retired

June 10–11, Le Mans 24 Hours, France

Gurney/Foyt	1st	*MK IV*	
McLaren/Donohue	4th	*MK IV*	
Andretti/Bianchi	—	*MK IV*	retired
Ruby/Hulme	—	*MK IV*	retired
Hawkins/Bucknum	—	*MK IIB*	retired
Gardner/McCluskey	—	*MK IIB*	retired
Schlesser/Ligier	—	*MK IIB*	retired
Ickx/Muir	—	*MIRAGE*	retired
Piper/Thompson	—	*MIRAGE*	retired
Maglioli/Casoni	—	*GT 40*	retired
Salmon/Redman	—	*GT 40*	retired
Greder/Dumay	—	*GT 40*	retired

June 18, Auvergne Trophy, Clermont-Ferrand, France

Hawkins	1st	*GT 40*
Sutcliffe	2d	*GT 40*
Schlesser	3d	*GT 40*

June 24–25, Reims 12 Hours, France

Schlesser/Ligier	1st	*MK II*	
Bond/Sutcliffe	7th	*GT 40*	
Pierpoint/Crabbe	8th	*GT 40*	
Nelson/Liddell	12th	*GT 40*	
Maglioli/Vaccarella	—	*GT 40*	retired
Greder/Giorgi	—	*GT 40*	retired

July 15, Group 4 Race, Silverstone, England

Liddell	2d	GT 40	
Crabbe	5th	GT 40	
Drury	6th	GT 40	
Fry	7th	GT 40	
Hawkins	—	GT 40	retired
Nelson	—	GT 40	retired

July 23, Circuito di Mugello, Italy

Schlesser/Ligier	4th	MK II
Nelson	13th	GT 40

July 30, BOAC Trophy, Brands Hatch, England

Liddell/Gethin	12th	GT 40	
Drury/Holland	14th	GT 40	
Sutton/Bond	16th	GT 40	
Rodriguez/Thompson	—	MIRAGE	retired
Lucas/Pike	—	GT 40	retired
Crabbe/Charlton	—	GT 40	retired

August 13, Wills Trophy, Croft, England

Liddell	4th	GT 40	
Drury	5th	GT 40	
De Klerk	6th	GT 40	
Sutcliffe	—	GT 40	retired

August 20, Austrian Grand Prix, Zeltweg, Austria

Hawkins	1st	*GT 40*	
Vaccarella/Maglioli	3d	*GT 40*	
Nelson	5th	*GT 40*	
Neerpasch-Crabbe	—	*GT 40*	retired
Hulme/Lucas	—	*GT 40*	retired

August 28, Group 4 Race, Brands Hatch, England

Hawkins	2d	*GT 40*	
Liddell	5th	*GT 40*	
Sutcliffe	6th	*GT 40*	
Prophet	7th	*GT 40*	
Lucas	—	*GT 40*	retired

September 9, Holts Trophy, Crystal Palace, England

Drury	6th	*GT 40*

September 16, Group 4 Race, Oulton Park, England

Hawkins	1st	*GT 40*	
Bond	5th	*GT 40*	
Hobbs	—	*GT 40*	retired
Corner	—	*GT 40*	retired
Humble	—	*GT 40*	retired

September 24, GT Race, Mallory Park, England

Nelson	2d	*GT 40*

September 30, Group 6 Race, Skarpnack, Sweden

Bonnier	1st	*MIRAGE*
Hawkins	2d	*MIRAGE*

October 15, 1,000 Km of Paris, Montlhery, France

Ickx/Hawkins	1st	*MIRAGE*	
Schlesser/Ligier	4th	*MK II*	
Giorgi/Jabouille	—	*GT 40*	retired
Vaccarella/Maglioli	—	*GT 40*	retired
Corner/Blades	—	*GT 40*	retired

November 4, Kyalami 9 Hours, South Africa

Ickx/Redman	1st	*MIRAGE*
Hailwood/Nelson	3d	*GT 40*

In 1967 Ford was 1st in the International Sports Car Championship.

Performance of the GT's and Prototypes

1964

Nürburgring 1,000 Km		**Laps**	**1**	**2**	**3**	**4**	**5**	**6**	
GT 40	P. Hill/McLaren		2	4	4	4	4	4	

Le Mans 24 Hours		**Hours**	**1**	**2**	**3**	**4**	**5**	**6**
GT 40	P. Hill/McLaren		44	38	28	23	17	13
GT 40	Ginther/Gregory		1	2	2	2	26	—
GT 40	Attwood/Schlesser		8	9	6	6	—	—

1965

Sebring		**Hours**	**1**	**2**	**3**	**4**	**5**	**6**	**7**
GT 40	McLaren/Miles		5	4	4	3	3	3	3

Targa Florio		**Laps**	**1**	**2**	**3**	**4**	**5**
GT SPYDER	Whitmore/Bondurant		3	4	3	4	13

Laps	7	8	9	10	11	12	13	14	15	16	
	4	4	4	4	4	4	4	4	5	—	Suspension

Hours	7	8	9	10	11	12	13	14	
	8	6	5	5	5	5	4	—	Gearbox
	—	—	—	—	—	—	—	—	Gearbox
	—	—	—	—	—	—	—	—	Fire

Hours	8	9	10	11	12
	2	2	2	2	2

Laps	6	7	8	9	10	
	12	10	9	—	—	Crash

Nürburgring 1,000 Km

		Laps	1	2	3	4	5	6	7	8
GT 40	Amon/Bucknum		4	5	5	5	5	5	4	4
GT 40	Whitmore/Attwood		17	12	9	8	8	8	7	6
GT 40	Trintignant/Ligier		27	23	17	15	15	13	12	11
*GT 40	McLaren/P. Hill		2	2	2	2	2	2	—	—

	Laps	26	27	28	29	30	31	32	33
Amon/Bucknum		14	14	14	13	10	10	10	9
Whitmore/Attwood		5	6	6	7	7	7	6	10
Trintignant/Ligier		—	—	—	—	—	—	—	—
McLaren/P. Hill		—	—	—	—	—	—	—	—

*The McLaren/P. Hill car had an engine displacement of 5,300 cc; the other Fords had the normal 4,727 cc.

Le Mans 24 Hours

		Hours	1	2	3	4
MK II	P. Hill/Amon		2	35	31	26
GT 40	Whitmore/Ireland		11	7	9	24
MK II	McLaren/Miles		1	1	6	—
GT 40	Bondurant/Maglioli		5	17	—	—
GT 40	Trintignant/Ligier		45	—	—	—

Fastest race lap: Phil Hill 3 min. 37.5 sec., 138.4 mph (new record).
Fastest practice lap: Phil Hill 3 min. 33.0 sec., 141.4 mph.

Laps	9	10	11	12	13	14	15	16	17	18	19	20	21	22	23	24	25
	4	3	3	3	3	3	3	21	21	19	18	18	18	15	14	13	13
	6	5	5	5	5	5	4	4	4	3	3	3	3	3	3	3	3
	10	8	8	7	7	7	7	12	12	11	10	10	10	20	—	—	—
	—	—	—	—	—	—	—	—	—	—	—	—	—	—	—	—	—

Laps	34	35	36	37	38	39	40	41	42	43	44	
	10	9	9	8	8	8	8	8	8	8	—	One lap behind
	9	—	—	—	—	—	—	—	—	—	—	Engine bracket
	—	—	—	—	—	—	—	—	—	—	—	Gear selector
	—	—	—	—	—	—	—	—	—	—	—	Halfshaft

Hours	5	6	7	8	
	24	21	—	—	Gearbox
	22	—	—	—	Overheating
	—	—	—	—	Gearbox
	—	—	—	—	Head gasket
	—	—	—	—	Gearbox

1966

Daytona Continental 24 Hours		Start 3:00 p.m.	6:00 p.m.	9:00 p.m.	10:45 p.m.
MK II	Miles/Ruby	1	1	1	1
MK II	Gurney/Grant	11	3	3	3
MK II	Hansgen/Donohue	3	2	2	2
MK II	McLaren/Amon	7	8	4	5
GT 40	Sutcliffe/Grossman	19	14	12	10
GT 40	Revson/Gregory	15	12	10	8
GT 40	Scott/Thompson/Revson	10	7	9	5
MK II (Aut)	Bucknum/Ginther	6	9	7	6
GT 40	Wonder/Wetanson	27	21	27	26

Winners: Miles/Ruby, 2,750.63 miles at 108.02 mph average. Fastest lap and new record: Dan Gurney, 1 min. 57.7 sec., 116.51 mph average.

Midnight	1:30 a.m.	5:00 a.m.	7:45 a.m.	11:45 a.m.	12:45 p.m.	1:40 p.m.	Finish 3:00 p.m.	
1	1	1	1	1	1	1	1	
3	3	3	3	2	2	2	2	
2	2	2	2	3	3	3	3	
5	5	5	5	5	5	5	5	
11	13	9	12	9	9	9	14	
8	10	11	8	10	11	15	17	
6	6	6	6	—	—	—	—	Brakes
14	21	17	—	—	—	—	—	Gearbox
36	43	—	—	—	—	—	—	Wheel trouble

Sebring 12 Hours

		Start	**1**	**2**	**3**
MK II XI	*Miles/Ruby*	5	2	2	2
MK II	*Hansgen/Donohue*	4	6	13	8
GT 40	*Revson/Scott*	13	11	8	9
MK II (Aut)	*Foyt/Bucknum*	10	9	37	30
GT 40	*Holquist/Jennings*	23	31	18	19
MK II	*Gurney/Grant*	1	3	1	1
GT 40	*Wonder*	26	25	21	21
GT 40	*Whitmore/Gardner*	7	8	6	6
GT 40	*G. Hill/Stewart*	3	4	4	4
GT 40	*Weitzes/Fisher*	22	19	15	18
GT 40	*McLean/Oulette*	16	16	10	13
GT 40	*Sutcliffe/Ireland*	20	12	22	35
GT 40	*Pabst/Gregory*	14	61	57	—

Winners: Miles/Ruby, 1,185.6 miles at 98.62 mph average. Fastest lap and new lap record: Dan Gurney, 2 min. 54.8 sec., 107.89 mph average.

Targa Florio

		Laps	**1**	**2**	**3**	**4**	**5**	**6**
GT 40	*Greder/Ligier*		11	10	12	14	12	8

4	5	6	7	8	9	10	11	12	
3	3	3	2	2	3	2	2	1	
18	11	19	13	11	6	5	3	2	
9	8	15	11	9	7	6	4	3	
31	39	36	30	23	18	16	15	12	
15	12	18	19	21	21	20	20	13	
1	1	1	1	1	1	1	1	—	Disqualified
19	24	33	32	38	36	—	—	—	Disqualified
5	5	8	6	5	—	—	—	—	Clutch
8	13	12	9	12	—	—	—	—	Valve
14	16	—	—	—	—	—	—	—	Withdrawn
12	22	—	—	—	—	—	—	—	Crash
49	38	—	—	—	—	—	—	—	Gasket
—	—	—	—	—	—	—	—	—	Engine

Laps	7	8	9	10	
	5	4	4	—	Crash

Nürburgring 1,000 Km

		Laps	**Start**	**1**	**2**	**3**	**4**	**5**	**6**
GT 40	*Ligier/Schlesser*		13	10	14	16	17	14	14
GT 40	*Sutcliffe/Taylor*		20	14	16	14	15	16	16
GT 40	*Bond/Spence*		17	18	18	21	21	21	22
GT 40	*Ireland/Salmon*		14	8	9	9	10	10	10
GT 40	*Scott/Revson*		15	9	10	10	11	—	—
GT 40	*Whitmore/Neerpasch*		10	—	—	—	—	—	—

	Laps	**23**	**24**	**25**	**26**	**27**	**28**	**29**
Ligier/Schlesser		9	9	9	8	7	6	6
Sutcliffe/Taylor		12	12	11	10	10	8	9
Bond/Spence		18	16	16	16	16	14	14
Ireland/Salmon		—	—	—	—	—	—	—
Scott/Revson		—	—	—	—	—	—	—
Whitmore/Neerpasch		—	—	—	—	—	—	—

7	8	9	10	11	12	13	14	15	16	17	18	19	20	21	22
13	11	11	10	9	7	7	7	7	9	9	10	9	9	9	9
15	15	14	13	12	11	10	10	12	12	12	13	13	13	12	13
20	21	21	21	21	21	19	18	18	17	17	17	16	16	15	18
9	8	9	11	10	9	8	—	—	—	—	—	—	—	—	—
—	—	—	—	—	—	—	—	—	—	—	—	—	—	—	—
—	—	—	—	—	—	—	—	—	—	—	—	—	—	—	—

30	31	32	33	34	35	36	37	38	39	40	41	42	43	44	
6	6	6	6	6	6	6	5	5	5	5	5	5	5	—	One lap behind
12	12	12	13	11	10	9	6	6	6	6	6	6	6	—	One lap behind
15	15	15	15	15	14	14	12	12	12	12	12	12	—	—	Two laps behind
—	—	—	—	—	—	—	—	—	—	—	—	—	—	—	Crash
—	—	—	—	—	—	—	—	—	—	—	—	—	—	—	Oil leak
—	—	—	—	—	—	—	—	—	—	—	—	—	—	—	Lost wheel

Le Mans 24 Hours

		Hours Start	1	2	3	4	5	6
MK II	*McLaren/Amon*	4	8	8	8	4	5	5
MK II	*Miles/Hulme*	2	5	2	1	1	1	3
MK II	*Bucknum/Hutcherson*	9	3	4	6	7	8	9
MK II	*Gurney/Grant*	1	1	1	4	2	2	4
GT 40	*Sutcliffe/Spoerry*	19	18	17	15	15	16	14
GT 40	*Grossman/Ligier*	20	15	15	16	16	15	17
GT 40	*Scott/Revson*	13	13	11	11	10	10	10
GT 40	*Ickx/Neerpasch*	14	13	12	13	13	13	13
MK II	*G. Hill/Muir*	6	2	5	9	6	7	10
MK II	*Bianchi/Andretti*	12	10	9	7	9	9	6
MK II	*Whitmore/Gardner*	3	34	34	47	47	45	—
MK II	*Hawkins/Donohue*	11	55	51	49	30	—	—
GT 40	*Ireland/Rindt*	17	51	52	—	—	—	—

1967

Sebring 12 Hours

		Hours 1	2	3	4	5
MK II	*Andretti/McLaren*	1	1	2	1	1
MK II	*Foyt/Ruby*	2	4	3	2	3
GT 40	*Maglioli/Vaccarella*	11	15	11	9	8
GT 40	*Grossman/McNamara*	18	13	15	12	12

Targa Florio

		Laps 1	2	3	4	5
GT 40	*Greder/Giorgi*	20	15	12	10	11
GT 40	*Schlesser/Ligier*	15	11	35	—	—

7	8	9	10	11	12	13	14	15	16	17	18	19	20	21	22	23	24	
5	4	4	3	3	3	3	3	3	1	3	1	1	1	1	2	2	1	
1	1	2	1	1	1	1	2	2	3	2	2	2	2	2	1	1	2	
10	9	5	5	4	4	4	4	4	4	3	3	3	3	3	3	3	3	
3	2	1	2	2	2	2	1	1	2	1	—	—	—	—				Water leak
13	11	10	10	8	6	7	7	6	5	—	—	—	—	—	—			Crash
15	16	13	12	11	8	11	11	12	—	—	—	—	—	—				Distributor
11	10	8	8	6	5	5	5	—	—	—	—	—	—	—	—			Camshaft
12	11	7	7	—	—	—	—	—	—	—	—	—	—	—	—			Engine
7	9	—	—	—	—	—	—	—	—	—	—	—	—	—	—			Front suspension
21	—	—	—	—	—	—	—	—	—	—	—	—	—	—	—			Engine
—	—	—	—	—	—	—	—	—	—	—	—	—	—	—				Transmission
—	—	—	—	—	—	—	—	—	—	—	—	—	—	—				Transmission
—	—	—	—	—	—	—	—	—	—	—	—	—	—	—	—			Engine

6	7	8	9	10	11	12
1	1	1	1	1	1	1
3	3	2	2	2	2	2
10	7	4	4	4	5	5
11	12	10	8	7	8	8

6	7	8	9	
10	10	7	6	1st in class
—	—	—	—	Crash

Nürburgring 1,000 Km

		Laps Start	1	2	3	4	5	6
GT 40	Greder/Giorgi	17	16	16	16	15	14	14
GT 40	Crabbe/Pierpoint	21	18	18	17	18	16	15
GT 40	Schlesser/Ligier	13	30	69	67	64	59	56
GT 40	Nelson/deKlerk	20	20	17	18	16	15	16

	Laps	24	25	26	27	28	29	30
	Greder/Giorgi	10	10	9	10	10	10	9
	Crabbe/Pierpoint	9	9	11	9	9	9	8
	Schlesser/Ligier	13	13	12	11	19	18	17
	Nelson/deKlerk	—	—	—	—	—	—	—

Le Mans 24 Hours

		Hours 1	2	3	4	5	6	7
MK IV	Gurney/Foyt	2	1	1	1	1	1	1
MK IV	McLaren/Donohue	3	4	3	4	2	2	3
MK II	Bucknum/Hawkins	1	42	35	25	23	22	19
GT 40	Greder/Dumay	17	19	28	42	38	37	31
MK IV	Andretti/Bianchi	8	3	7	2	3	6	5
MK IV	Gardner/McCluskey	11	8	6	9	14	13	11
MK II	Schlesser/Ligier	7	9	9	7	7	7	6
GT 40	Maglioli/Casoni	15	14	16	16	18	18	20
MK IV	Ruby/Hulme	30	27	18	26	36	32	35
MIRAGE	Piper/Thompson	28	18	22	21	—	—	—
MIRAGE	Ickx/Muir	16	35	46	—	—	—	—
GT 40	Salmon/Redman	21	—	—	—	—	—	—

7	8	9	10	11	12	13	14	15	16	17	18	19	20	21	22	23
13	13	13	13	12	10	11	14	14	14	13	13	11	11	11	11	10
14	14	14	14	13	12	12	13	13	12	11	11	10	10	10	10	9
52	46	44	38	33	31	24	22	18	17	15	15	14	14	14	14	13
15	15	39	37	31	30	25	25	24	25	24	23	20	19	18	17	—

31	32	33	34	35	36	37	38	39	40	41	42	43	44	
9	8	8	8	8	7	7	7	7	7	7	7	—	—	
7	7	7	7	7	8	8	8	8	8	8	8	—	—	
17	16	14	14	13	11	11	11	10	—	—	—	—	—	
—	—	—	—	—	—	—	—	—	—	—	—	—	—	Oil pressure

8	9	10	11	12	13	14	15	16	17	18	19	20	21	22	23	24	
1	1	1	1	1	1	1	1	1	1	1	1	1	1	1	1	1	
2	2	2	3	5	6	5	5	5	4	4	4	4	4	4	4	4	
15	12	12	12	11	9	7	6	6	6	—	—	—	—				Oil lack
28	23	21	19	17	15	—	—	—	—	—	—	—	—				Oil pressure
4	3	3	2	7	—	—	—	—	—	—	—	—	—				Crash
11	10	10	9	12	—	—	—	—	—	—	—	—	—				Crash
5	6	5	6	9	—	—	—	—	—	—	—	—	—				Crash
18	—	—	—	—	—	—	—	—	—	—	—	—	—				Engine
—	—	—	—	—	—	—	—	—	—	—	—	—	—				Trapped in sand
—	—	—	—	—	—	—	—	—	—	—	—	—	—				Engine
—	—	—	—	—	—	—	—	—	—	—	—	—	—				Connecting rod
—	—	—	—	—	—	—	—	—	—	—	—	—	—				Crash